# MYTHS
## — of the —
# asanas

# MYTHS
## — of the —
# asanas

## THE STORIES AT THE HEART OF THE YOGA TRADITION

Alanna Kaivalya, Ph.D. & Arjuna van der Kooij

Foreword by Shiva Rea • Afterword by Manorama

Illustrations by Chris Yeazel

**MANDALA**
PUBLISHING

*San Rafael, California*

**MANDALA**
PUBLISHING

www.mandalaearth.com

Copyright © 2010 Alanna Kaivalya and Arjuna van der Kooij
Foreword © 2010 Shiva Rea
Afterword © 2010 Manorama
Illustrations © 2010 Chris Yeazel

Library of Congress Cataloging-in-Publication Data available.

ISBN: 978-1-60109-057-7

ROOTS of PEACE    REPLANTED PAPER

Insight Editions, in association with Roots of Peace, will plant two trees for
each tree used in the manufacturing of this book. Roots of Peace is an internationally
renowned humanitarian organization dedicated to eradicating land mines worldwide and
converting war-torn lands into productive farms and wildlife habitats. Together, we will
plant two million fruit and nut trees in Afghanistan and provide farmers there with the
skills and support necessary for sustainable land use.

Manufactured in China by Insight Editions
www.insighteditions.com

10 9 8

Designed by Dagmar Trojanek & Barbara Genetin

*To I. L. M.*

*Govindam adi purusham tam aham bhajami*

# contents

# foreword

**Y**OGA IS MYTHIC. It is a reflection of the cosmic forces that are timeless and universal in nature—creation, continuity, and dissolution—which are embodied in yoga as asanas and mudras. You don't need to travel to India to feel the coiled power of a cobra, or *bhujangasana*, in your body, or the rooted power of a tree in *vrikshasana*. But few Westerners know the stories behind the names of the asanas or of the all-pervasive nature of the Shiva and Ganesha myths that are known by everyone in India, from children to the gurus. Most all traditional Indian songs, dances, and visual arts are depictions of myths. Myths are special teachers. They are sometimes mysterious, contradictory, peaceful, wrathful, and liberating at their core.

*What is the somatic feeling of tearing open your heart as the monkey god Hanuman? Who are the great sages Bharadvaja and Astavakra, whom the asanas are named after? What is the significance of* Natarajasana, *or the lord of the dance pose?*

When you learn the stories of the asanas, you are entering a space of mythic consciousness, the place where you no longer need to know the outer asana—those remarkable moving mudras—but the *inner* asana, or the landscape to which the myth refers.

My father gave me my name, Shiva, when he was an art student. He had never attended a yoga class before and was truly inspired by the myths of Shiva, the matted-hair cosmic dancer decimating ignorance with the sublime grace and power of his *Ananda Tandava*, or dance of bliss, a great archetype for the late sixties. As a seven-year-old growing up in Berkeley in 1974 at the heart of Vietnam Protest, I looked out into the world and felt the heaviness of cosmic destruction. For most of my childhood, I actually thought that I was named after the lord of destruction, which was the common definition in encyclopedias and dictionaries. I didn't have a book or a teacher at that time to reveal the inner meanings of the name. I now know there are a thousand names for Shiva—ranging from the peaceful and sublime Mahayogin, from which all the yogic asanas emerged; to the lover of Shakti, Kamadeva; to the great howler, Rudra.

I have fallen madly in love with the goddess and have been anchored during the storms of my life in the myths of the great goddess Durga, who, accompanied by her army of sixty-four thousand yoginis, enters places of utter chaos and resurrects the world through her fierce love. I consider myself a peaceful, simple, nature-loving person, and yet there is something so wild and intensely satisfying about these yogic myths that shatters our rigid, conservative, and shallow ideas about our divine nature and truly meets us in the light and dark of our being and life path.

Alanna Kaivalya and Arjuna van der Kooij have offered you a treasure in *Myths of the Asanas* from the depth of their personal realizations as yogic practitioners and kirtan artists. They have lived this terrain in their own hearts and lives as well as in the context in which myth is perpetually reflected. I have great respect for David Life and Sharon Gannon, and for Alanna's training as a Jivamukti teacher, for this method has brought *satsang*—the sharing of truth through yoga's wisdom teachings—into the landscape of asana practice. If you are a yoga practitioner, you will bathe in the mythic wisdom of this book.

However, if you know nothing of the asanas, you will also benefit from these powerful myths. They have sustained the flow of yoga since the earliest recorded written history. These myths are some of the most profound understandings of universal consciousness. Even Einstein was deeply influenced by the creation myths of Nataraja as a reflection of his discoveries of quantum physics.

I hope you will enjoy this gemlike book as much as I have, as it is a resource to have at your fingertips to gradually absorb the power of these teachings into your own consciousness and evolution in yoga practice. This is a wonderful book for yoga teachers, and I finally have a great resource to direct my own teacher trainees for further study.

Jai Sri Ganesha and his sacred tusk, which was used to help Vyasa record some of these myths from the Mahabharata.

Jai Mandala Publishing for continuing to support such works as *Myths of the Asanas*.

Blessings to all travelers on this meandering road of life.

SHIVA REA
*Costa Rica, 2010*

# introduction

THE GIFTS OF YOGA are as numerous and varied as the petals of a lotus blossom. Although yoga's broader teachings touch on all aspects of life, it is asana practice that has made it immensely popular around the globe, and there is a good reason for it. Asana practice challenges the body and focuses the mind, while its philosophical principles encourage spiritual growth. Asanas can be viewed as a kind of prayer, and they have a significant and wholesome effect on our physical body, our psyche, and our emotional health. This distinguishes asana practice from other systematized forms of movement.

This book provides the background myths for about thirty asanas. Asanas are often named after some ancient yogic sage, deity, or sacred animal. The myths behind the asanas are intended to serve as inspirational guides that can enhance our yoga practice, fueling it with a deeper, meditative quality. They provide us with a fresh perspective on ourselves, helping us connect our everyday lives with yoga through the postures.

All of the stories in this book illustrate some mystical, hidden potential within us. This potential tends to lie dormant until we illuminate it with awareness. To be mystical is to look within oneself for the source of all that is. In this sense the essence of the stories is found within the experience of our own hearts.

Each of the characters in the myths displays human flaws, which make them easy to relate to. So as we read about the uncertainty of Hanuman before making his leap across the ocean, we are invited to think about the moments in our life when we felt the same way, when we called into question our potential and doubted our ability to achieve something we thought was not possible.

These myths have been told since ancient times. Whether or not they actually happened is of less importance than the symbolic meaning they convey. The myths of ancient India concern themselves with the transformation of consciousness. Yoga and mythology scholar Mircea Eliade defined myths as "dramatic breakthroughs of the sacred into the world." He noted that the language of myth does not argue, but simply presents. The myths of yoga's spiritual tradition have the power to change old patterns of behavior, providing us with enlightened insight that brings us closer to who we really are. And this is precisely what the yoga tradition is concerned with. As Ecknath Easwaran put it, "yogic myth has a genius to clothe the *infinite* in human form."

The myths point to a higher state of consciousness. They depict the travel of the soul from ignorance to illumination. Their goal is to take us from the illusions of our ego-centered existence (*samsara*) to the reality of liberated existence, which has three main components: truth (*sat*), clear consciousness (*cit*), and boundless joy (*ananda*).

The myths behind the asanas have much to teach us. Meditating on the tolerance of trees can actually inspire us to become more tolerant. Hearing about how the disfigured Astavakra came to be the teacher of a king can diminish our concern with our external appearance and our self-imposed limitations. Marveling at the devotion of Hanuman can help us gain some of the spiritual strength and determination he represents. Through the myths, the asanas can become true vehicles for transformation. We hope this book will help you add a new dimension to your practice, understanding, and love of yoga.

# poses of the yogi

Padmasana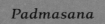

Siddhasana

Anjali & Namaste Mudras

Dhanurasana

Chakrasana

Balasana

Trikonasana

Dandasana

S IMPLY PUT, YOGIS EMBODY THE WORLD. Using their bodies as tools, yogis put themselves into certain positions in order to understand the workings of the world around them. By doing so, they gain empathy, compassion, and sensitivity—qualities that contribute to a more elevated state of mind, known as *chitta prasadanam* in yogic scripture.

The literal meaning of the Sanskrit word *yoga* is "yoking" or "connecting." One way of describing the state of yoga is as a feeling of interconnectedness, in which we experience that a part of us exists in everything and vice versa. To understand this more fully, we try to resemble everything we know in the universe through our asana practice. This exploration can be likened to a story about King Arthur. As a young prince, Arthur thought that the most enjoyable part of becoming king would be to rule over his kingdom. The wizard Merlin decided that Arthur would benefit from a powerful lesson. He changed the boy into different people, animals, and objects found within his kingdom, such as a peasant, a fish, a tree, the water, and a rock, so that Prince Arthur could understand what it was actually like to *be* those different beings and things. Arthur's experiences gave him the much-needed ability to put himself in others' shoes. He began to understand that the most important job of being king is not to rule, but to serve.

Asana practice has a similar goal. We take the shape of the tree, the fish, the warrior, the turtle, and the sage so that we can begin to understand their essential natures. We can literally feel the wisdom of the sage and the stability of the tree. We can feel the power of the warrior and the steadfastness of the turtle. As a result, we experience ourselves as more deeply connected with all of life around us. Through asana practice we can feel that our body is a microcosm of the universe.

The yogi is ready and willing to embody all states of existence, including ones that usually repulse mere mortals, such as snakes, scorpions, and even death. Through yoga, we come to know the other as ourselves and ourselves as the other. The practice allows us the opportunity to dissolve the separation born from ego, along with the fear, cynicism, and isolation that sometimes go along with daily life. Feeling joy in coming to know the world, the journey of the yogi begins.

# padmasana

## LOTUS POSE

The lotus posture is the quintessential seated meditation posture, which often eludes yogis whose hips have not yet softened through their asana practice. With the feet crossed on top of the thighs, this posture pins the thighbones to the floor, creating a grounded seat and an effortlessly straight spine. The lotus is a potent symbol for the yogi and is often associated with the creative forces within us. Another powerful symbol of creativity is the sound of OM.

## ~⊃ Cosmic Soup

Before the dawn of time, Vishnu was resting comfortably on his couch—the thousand-headed serpent Ananta. Coiled underneath Vishnu, Ananta provided a suitable lounging place, while his numerous heads provided shelter and shade for the reclining deity. Vishnu and Ananta floated together on the cosmic sea of possibility, where all the universes enter after the cosmic annihilation. When the moment came for the creation cycle to start again, a grand lotus flower began to sprout from Vishnu's navel.

The plant grew up right in front of him, and then the beautiful lotus flower opened to reveal the four faces of Brahma, the god of creation, nestled inside. Each of the faces was looking in one of the cardinal directions—north, south, east, and west. From each of his four mouths, Brahma uttered one of the four parts of the sacred sound of OM: "ah," "ooo," "mmm," and silence. The sound caused the cosmic ocean to begin swirling and congealing into the universe as we know it today.

OM is the epitome of possibility. It is from this sound that all possibilities arise. According to one theory, the four parts of OM represent the cycle that everything must pass through. The first part, "ah" (as in "father"), represents creation or birth. The second part, "ooo" (as in "room"), symbolizes sustenance or life. The third part, "mmm," represents destruction or death. These three parts are presided over by the cosmic trinity of Brahma, Vishnu, and Shiva.

The fourth part, which is considered the most important, is the sound of silence. The moment after OM is uttered, we listen. The silence represents the complete resolution of the previous three parts. In yogic terms, this resolution could be described as oneness,

enlightenment, or simply as yoga. It is customary to begin and end yoga classes with the sound of OM.

It is no coincidence that the seat for this creative sound is the unstained flower of the lotus, which represents purity and perfection. The lotus grew from Vishnu's navel. The navel is also the place from which we were fed while in our mother's womb as we grew into a baby and ultimately the person we are today.

# ～◌ The Symbol of the Lotus

All over India the iconic lotus flower grows in canals and swamps—even the most heavily polluted ones. Despite its regal blossom, the lotus comes from humble beginnings. Its seed is planted in muck at the bottom of a murky pond. Although far beneath the surface of the water, the lotus root takes hold, and the shoot starts to search for the sun. Symbolically, the sun represents illuminated knowledge, or ultimate truth.

Rays of light refract as they move through water. This is what causes a straw to look bent in a glass of water. This refraction makes it challenging to see the sun clearly from beneath the surface of the water, but the lotus still knows it has to rise up through the water to catch the clearest rays. Once on top of the water, the blooming lotus takes care that none of its petals touch the murky water. It opens its pink petals and turns its face to the light in a simple gesture, rejoicing in its discovery. Looking at the flower, one would have no idea that it came from such murky beginnings.

The journey of this sacred flower reflects the journey of the yogi. We are rooted in the earth, absorbed by the endless cycle of births, deaths, sicknesses, tragedies, celebrations, bills, apartment leases, and family relations. The yogi knows this muck as the dirt of *avidya*, the great mistake of identifying ourselves with something other than our divine nature. According to Patanjali's Yoga Sutra, avidya is one of the greatest obstacles on the path to self-realization. We define ourselves by our names, careers, family history, illnesses, injuries, age, race, religion, and all the things that separate us from one another. We say, "I am a woman, you are a man," or "I am American and you are Iraqi." If we are not careful, these definitions and labels keep us mired more deeply in the muck of duality, and we fail to see others and ourselves as being a part of one whole. This kind of thinking represents exclusivity, whereas yoga seeks to join or include all beings, no matter how they define themselves.

Much like the lotus seed, we may often feel stuck in this muck of labels and separateness. Then by chance, we may receive a little wisdom. Maybe on an off day, like the tumultuous day on the stormy sea that Vishnu experienced, we hear some simple wisdom that cracks open the tough shell of the little lotus seed. And so our journey begins. From there we move through the distorting water of our limited understanding and reach for the light of wisdom, which is always shining on us, if only we would take the time to notice it. The promise of yoga is that eventually, through enough nurturing and determination, we will surface above the water and realize our full potential.

Grandiose? Sure. But lotuses bloom all the time. They bloom all over the world, and they don't make a big deal about it. They know that to bloom is their ultimate goal and that it's worth continuously reaching through the distortion to find the ultimate source of light. The struggle is just part of the process, and the result is pure beauty.

As the ultimate seated posture, *padmasana* engages us in the higher yoga practices of concentration, meditation, and ultimately samadhi, or enlightenment. By sitting in this position, we are connected firmly to the earth and our roots. As our practice grows, and our consciousness begins to ascend, we sit tall, just like the lotus reaching through the water to bloom in the sun. As with the lotus, our humble beginnings need not prevent us from blossoming in purity.

# anjali & namaste mudras

*Anjali* and *namaste mudras* are not asanas, but rather energetic seals, or symbolic gestures, which are commonly used in asana practice. At the beginning of practice, we typically bring our hands together in a prayer position while chanting OM. Those who practice vinyasa-style asana will bring their hands to prayer at the start and close of sun salutations as well as in warrior 1, with arms raised overhead. This gesture is a touchstone of the practice and has such a potent meaning that its origin is worth a closer look.

## ⌒⊃ Patanjali

As the grand preserving force of the universe, Vishnu watches carefully to see when we need a course correction here on earth. Any time he sees civil unrest, general unhappiness, or a unique opportunity for the human race to advance, he will show up on earth to help us out. We've seen his manifestations in great figures like King Ram and Krishna. At one point, he looked at the earth and saw that there was an opportunity to bring more cohesion into the lives of people who were interested in yoga.

About two thousand years ago, there were many factions among those who practiced yoga. Lying on the great serpent Ananta on the great ocean of possibility, Vishnu noticed this separateness in the practice of yoga, and he thought it would be a good idea to find a way to bring everyone together. He decided to send his liaison Ananta, charging the thousand-headed serpent with the task of bringing the yoga groups together into one great practice.

Down on earth lived a lovely woman who had the misfortune of being unable to have children. She was a devout worshipper of Vishnu and prayed every day for the miracle of a child. As she prayed, she held her hands open to receive any grace that might fall upon her. She waited and hoped and never gave up.

One day, as she was down on her knees with upturned hands reaching toward the sky, Vishnu decided to let the grace of his grand serpent fall upon this sweet woman. Into her praying hands fell baby Patanjali. (*Pat* means "to fall" in Sanskrit, and *anjali* was the gesture the woman made with her hands.) This was no ordinary baby boy. He had the upper torso of a normal human, but his lower half was a snake's tail. Apparently Ananta didn't have time to make a complete transformation on his fall to earth. But who was the woman to question a gift from above? So she loved him and raised him as her own, despite his serpentine lower half.

Patanjali grew to be a great master of yoga, and he helped the world by uniting all the different ideas about yoga into one grand work, called the Yoga Sutra. *Sutra* means "thread," and this classic text consists of short aphorisms, which pull yoga together into one great fabric. Each little phrase encompasses great wisdom, which has sustained yoga for the last two thousand years. Patanjali's yoga sutras outline several different methods for achieving ultimate happiness, or yoga. The most well known of these is ashtanga yoga. The ashtanga yoga path includes *yama* (restraint), *niyama* (observances), *asana* (seat or posture), *pranayama* (breath work), *pratyahara* (turning inward), *dharana* (concentration), *dhyana* (meditation), and *samadhi* (enlightenment).

Praying with outstretched hands, in anjali mudra, symbolizes the unwavering belief that whatever one is praying for will soon arrive. Inherent in this gesture is a strong pulsation of faith, or *shraddha*. Faith is what is required to be able to make great leaps (as we'll see in the story of Hanuman on page 76) and receive great blessings, as Patanjali's mother did.

## ∾ Namaste—Reverence to Thee

While namaste and anjali are generally interchangeable names for a similar gesture, there is no myth associated with the namaste mudra. Namaste is a sort of variation on anjali that helps us in our efforts to find a balance. The word "namaste" is also an important and pervasive aspect of today's yoga practice. We end classes with the gesture of bringing our hands to prayer and the salutation "namaste." This is reflective of yoga's end goal.

Ultimately, yoga seeks to join all opposites and dissolve any illusion of separateness that may exist. Any time we weave the inhale into the exhale, look for similarities between ourselves and our partner, or watch as day slowly turns to night with no definitive break in between, we are experiencing the presence of yoga that is all around us. This process can be experienced internally, too, as described in another classic yoga text, the Hatha Yoga Pradipika.

In the Hatha Yoga Pradipika, the concept of duality is introduced as a sun and moon within the body, with the sun representing the right side of the body and the moon representing the left. The ultimate aim of asana practice is to use various methods to dissolve this opposition and allow all our energy to be unified. The goal is a feeling of true balance within the body and mind—a constant flow of energy, thought, and behavior that favors neither light nor dark, good nor bad, up nor down, lazy nor energetic. It is the opposition that actually shows us how to find balance, like a pendulum swinging from side to side that eventually comes to rest in the center. And for a yogi, the center is the heart.

During asana practice, we work and allow our energy to become balanced. Stretching our muscles creates the space for this to occur, as does deep and steady breathing. We remind ourselves of this search for balance by bringing our hands together in prayer in front of our heart. This is called the namaste mudra. Namaste means "obeisance to you" or "reverence to you," which can be more poetically translated as "the light in me honors the light in you." When we do this periodically throughout our practice, it becomes a touchstone for us to remember why we have come to our mat and what yoga means to us. Both anjali and namaste mudra represent the crux of yoga practice—two seemingly opposing forces (such as masculine-feminine, rational-emotional, sun-moon) being joined. In these gestures, we bring both the right and left sides of the body together at the heart.

# chakrasana

## WHEEL POSE

*Chakrasana*, or wheel pose, is a deep backbend. It is similar to *urdhva mukha dhanurasana* (upward-facing bow), except that in this pose, the hands "walk" close enough to the feet to grasp the ankles. When the hands and feet connect, the body resembles a wheel or circle. This circle represents the completion of our internal energy circuit, which begins at the energy center that is located at the base of the spine and ends at the energy center at the crown of the head.

In ashtanga yoga practice, chakrasana is a transitional movement that takes the practitioner from *halasana* (plow pose) to *chaturanga dandasana* (four-limbed staff pose). In this case, the name "chakrasana" refers to the turning of the body like a wheel, from one pose to the next.

## ⌣ The Wheel's Architect

In the yoga tradition, the grand architect of the universe is Vishwakarman. He is credited with designing the earth, the heavens, and outer space. He had a lovely daughter named Sanjana with a face as luminous as ten thousand moons. Sanjana fell in love with Surya, the sun god. Despite Sanjana's brightness, Surya outshone her, which made it impossible for her to get close to him. So she went to her father for help.

Vishwakarman decided to shave off enough of the sun's rays so that his daughter could easily stand next to her beloved without being blinded by his brightness. As the sparkling sunshine fell to the earth, Vishwakarman gathered it up and created a huge *chakra*, or spinning disk. His plan worked, and as Sanjana and Surya drew nearer to one another, their love grew stronger, and they became inseparable.

The same chakra that helped Sanjana win Surya's love serves as a formidable weapon for Vishnu, who uses it for his role as the protector of the universe. Vishnu casually twirls it around one finger, displaying his control over all that spins—the orbits of the heavenly bodies in the solar system, as well as the spinning wheels of energy, the seven chakras, which exist within our bodies.

## ⌣ Discovering the Wheels of Energy

During the fifteenth century, a group of renegade yogis, known as the Nath yogis, were among the first people to systemize and document the importance and function of the chakras in our bodies. They banded together to strengthen their skills as warriors through various physical yoga practices. They found that if they used their bodies to perform asanas, pranayama (breath work), specific mudras, and deep, inner listening, they could more easily

achieve *siddhis*, or yogic powers. These powers made them very desirable as warriors. Who wouldn't want warriors on their side in battle who could make themselves invisible or had the strength of an elephant?

The Nath yogis defined and perfected what we know today as *hatha* yoga. Hatha yoga has become an umbrella name for all the different yoga styles that focus on using the physical yoga practices (such as asana, pranayama, mudras, and deep listening) to reach enlightenment. One of the greatest Nath yogis of the time, named Swatmarama, gathered the results of their practice into the Hatha Yoga Pradipika. In this classic yoga text we find an in-depth exploration of how to use the tool of our body to calm and focus the mind.

In the Pradipika, yogis learn about the seven chakras, or energy centers, that operate in the body. We can think of the chakras as states of consciousness. As our consciousness ascends, we get closer and closer to the state of yoga.

These energy centers are called *chakras* because of their resemblance to spinning wheels. The speed at which each center spins depends on the level of energy within. The more energetic the chakra, the faster the spin. What we want is just the right amount of spin in order to feel balanced, like the earth spinning on its axis. When our energy is balanced, it is flowing in a natural and rhythmic state, which gives us a sense of stability and harmony.

## Centers of Energy

As we practice asanas and begin to energize or balance these centers, we feel the effect that each has on our lives. An imbalance in any of these centers may manifest physically. We may have trouble balancing in standing poses, experience indigestion, or become choked up in conversation. The chakras offer a key to what the body is trying to communicate. They help us address any issues that come up in our practice.

### MULADHARA CHAKRA

The root chakra is located at the base of the spine. Our legs and feet are its extensions. The *muladhara chakra* represents basic issues such as stability within the home and finances and our relationship to our parents. Physically, it governs the organs of elimination. Standing postures help to balance the muladhara chakra by providing a chance to improve our balance and create a stable base for us to stand on.

### SVADHISTHANA CHAKRA

The sacral chakra is underneath the navel on the sacrum and incorporates the pelvis. It represents our relationships (particularly sexual relationships), emotions, and our ability to be both creative and procreative. The svadhisthana chakra governs the sexual organs. Hip-opening postures help to balance the svadhisthana chakra by creating openness and receptivity in our emotional center, making us more available to relate to others and channel our creativity.

### MANIPURA CHAKRA

The power chakra is located at the solar plexus, near the middle of the spine. It represents individuality, ego, and how we present ourselves to the world. *Manipura chakra* influences how we conduct ourselves, particularly in our career and our relationships with our co-workers. It governs the organs of digestion. Twisting postures help to balance the manipura chakra by wringing out the ego, just as we would wring out a wet sponge.

### ANAHATA CHAKRA

The heart chakra is located in the chest and thorax and extends to the arms and hands. It represents our ability to give compassion and unconditional love to the world. The ability to forgive is located here, so relationships to those who may have harmed us are dealt with in this region. The *anahata chakra* governs breathing and our cardiovascular systems. Backbends help to balance anahata chakra by physically creating more openness in the heart, which enhances our ability to offer compassion to others.

### VISUDDHA CHAKRA

The communication chakra is located at the throat and includes the ears. It represents our ability to communicate and listen, and because our voice can be used to communicate love or hate, it affects our relationships with those we may have harmed. *Visuddha chakra* governs the thyroid and cervical spine. The shoulder stand, plow pose, and fish pose help to balance the visuddha chakra by placing pressure around the throat, encouraging any poisons or blockages to fall away.

### AJNA CHAKRA

The intuitive chakra is located at the third eye, between the eyebrows. It represents our ability to look upon our world with equanimity and see all beings as having something in common. We can best achieve these goals if we enjoy a good relationship to some higher power. The ajna chakra governs the pituitary gland. *Kapalabhati* (skull shining breath) and child's poses help to balance the *ajna chakra* by bringing energy to this place, allowing us to become more attentive to the unseen aspects of life.

## SAHASRARA CHAKRA

The crown chakra is located at the top of the head in the place where babies have a soft spot. This represents our deep connection to a divine source and our relationship to that source. The *sahasrara chakra* governs the pineal gland. Meditation and headstands help to balance the sahasrara chakra by giving us a steady connection to the divine source. (We connect to the divinity of the earth in headstand, and the divinity from above in meditation).

Learning about the function and location of each of these chakras informs our practice. If we know where we are stuck, we know where to turn our attention. The more attention we pay to our body's communication, the more balanced we become energetically.

Traditionally, as with building a structure, we begin by balancing the base and work our way up. The lessons of each of the chakras give us platforms to firmly stand on as we continuously lift our energy to the next spinning wheel. For example, when we secure a great home and become financially stable, we are in the right place to enter a relationship or begin a creative project. With a good family by our side, we can start to make a mark and secure a powerful place in the world.

We continue to build our lives up through this energetic system on our way to ultimate harmony, which is made possible through engaging in yoga practice and letting go of the subtle layers of misidentification around our soul. When we connect our hands to our ankles in chakrasana and open our spine, the energy is free to move clearly around our bodies, just as the spinning disk rests easily on Vishnu's finger.

# trikonasana

## TRIANGLE POSE

The three angles (*tri konas* in Sansrkit) of a triangle make it one of the strongest and most stable shapes in nature. In triangle pose, there are three triangle shapes made with the body: one with our legs and the floor, a second one underneath the side of the body with the arm and front leg, and the third connecting the top hand and two feet.

The triangle pose represents many sacred trinities in our world, such as the trinity of earth, space, and heavens or that of birth, life, and death. *Trikonasana* also symbolizes the three *gunas*, or qualities, that compose our bodies and minds.

## The Three Gunas

Understanding the gunas enhances our comprehension of our yoga practice and allows us navigate the world around us better, as they affect everything in the universe. *Tamas guna*, which arises from Shiva, is the quality of inertia or unconsciousness. It causes indifference and can have a destructive energy. *Rajas guna*, which comes from Brahma, is the quality of passion and creativity, which provides the creative energy we need for manifesting things. *Sattva guna*, from Vishnu, is the quality of lightness and consciousness, which is necessary to sustain harmonious living and maintain our enlightened awareness. These gunas come together to create *maya*, the world of illusion that we experience through our senses.

The gunas color every aspect of our existence. When we are feeling slow and sluggish, and it's hard to get out of bed, we are under the influence of tamas guna. When we are very excited about something, to the point of distraction, we are under the influence of rajas guna. And when we are feeling our yoga buzz, we are under the influence of sattva guna. To help us understand the gunas, yoga philosophy compares them to animals. The sloth corresponds to tamas, because it moves so slowly that moss grows on its back. The bull is like rajas guna because it paws the ground and snorts. The cow resembles sattva guna because of its peaceful nature.

One of the aims of yoga practice is to invite as much clarity (sattva) in our lives as possible, while avoiding ignorance (tamas) and agitation (rajas). Tamas and rajas are not inherently bad, though. We need some tamas to fall asleep, and we need some rajas to get us going. It is only when we have too much of either that they prevent us from reaching a more noble and harmonious state of being.

The practice of yoga aims to reach a state of elevated consciousness called *suddha sattva*, or pure goodness, in which all

dualities are united in absolute harmony. To reach this goal, a yogi must get beyond even sattva guna because it still binds the soul to material existence in a subtle way. Sattva remains connected to the ego and therefore perpetuates a false sense of self. For example, engaging in acts of charity is a sattvic activity, yet it usually reinforces the ego in a subtle way. While we might feel good about ourselves for having given some money to a good cause, in a suddha sattvic state of mind we give purely because of our gratitude for having received, with the full understanding that nothing really belongs to us in the first place.

Only when we break through the veil of maya do we reside solely in our divine nature. So when performing trikonasana, it's helpful to meditate on the solid foundation that we need in order to live a sattvic life and leave the world of maya behind.

## The War of Illusion

A powerful demon named Mahishasura had been wreaking havoc upon the gods and goddesses in the heavens, threatening to overthrow them. He managed to distract them constantly from their duties, turning their attention instead toward worldly and unlasting pleasures. Mahishasura's depravity was distressing Shiva, Brahma, and Vishnu, the sacred trinity in charge. In an effort to overcome Mahishasura's debauchery, the sacred trinity brought their energy together to create the great goddess, Mahamaya (also known as Durga), just as the gunas come together to create maya.

A fierce warrior, Mahamaya and her trusty lion lunged at the evil demon. The wily Mahishasura transformed into different creatures to try to defeat them. Though his shape changed, his evil intensity stayed the same, and it became a formidable fight. Mahamaya's lion swiped at Mahishasura's chest, weakening him a bit. Mahamaya drew one of her endless supply of arrows and shot it right into Mahishasura's flaming mouth. That made him cry out and fall to the ground. She promptly stood on top of him and used her scimitar to cut off his head, ending his evil reign. Having defeated the demon, Mahamaya restored light and grace to the heavens and to those who lived there.

In Sanskrit the words *maha maya* mean the "great illusion." Mahamaya fights against the constantly changing illusion that keeps us believing that what we see in the world is reality, rather than seeing the truth of what lies beneath it. Our minds work like the evil demon Mahishasura, creating many distractions to lead us away from our true nature, but Mahamaya works to keep us in touch with that true nature.

# siddhasana

## PERFECT POSE

*Siddhasana* means "perfect pose" or "pose of accomplishment." It is performed by placing the left heel against the groin area, or perineum, and the right ankle over the left. Together with padmasana and sukhasana, it is one of the postures recommended for use in pranayama and meditation. For *pranayama* (breath work) it is useful because it closes off the *muladhara*, or root chakra, with the heel, preventing the life force from escaping. It is called siddhasana because perfection, or *siddha*, in yoga is thought to be attainable by meditating in this posture.

## ꙅ Yogic Powers

"Siddha" refers to a yogi who has perfected yoga and achieved mastery over the gunas, so that his or her body and mind are composed primarily of the sattva guna, the quality of nature associated with lightness and consciousness. With this lightness, great powers, called siddhis, can be attained. The siddhis are discussed in the third chapter of the Yoga Sutra and include having the strength of an elephant, the ability to change size and shape, and the power to create objects at will.

Durvasa Muni was a renowned ascetic who had gained many such mystical powers. He was feared because of his hot temper and because he was quick to curse people. Durvasa could go without food for a hundred years, and he could later eat all the food he might have consumed over those hundred years in one meal.

Durvasa came to the court of King Ambarish, who was a fervent practitioner of yoga and a devotee of Vishnu. Durvasa agreed to be the king's guest and asked him to wait until he finished his bath at the river and returned. It so happened that Durvasa had come to Ambarish's court at the close of the king's day of fasting, which he had been observing for his spiritual benefit. It was prescribed that the king should break the fast before sunrise, but it would be disrespectful to eat any food before a guest had been fed. When the moment arrived for breaking fast, and Durvasa had still not returned from the river, the king had a dilemma. He resolved the problem by drinking a little water, which can be considered food, or not.

When Durvasa discovered the king had drunk some water before feeding him, he became enraged. With his mystical powers, he created a great demon, which he sent to ambush and kill King Ambarish. Although King Ambarish had many luxuries at his disposal, he was unattached to his wealth and kingdom,

knowing that none of it was permanent. Because of his simple-hearted devotion, he was protected by a cosmic weapon, the chakra of Vishnu.

As soon as the demon came near King Ambarish, the fearsome spinning wheel appeared and killed the demon instead. Then the chakra proceeded toward Durvasa, who fled the scene in great fear. Unable to shake off the spinning, scorching-hot chakra, Durvasa went to Shiva and Brahma for help, but to no avail. Finally he went to Vishnu, who told him, "There is nothing I can do. Only if my devotee, Ambarish, is willing to forgive you, may the chakra withdraw." Durvasa went back to the king and begged forgiveness.

The humble king readily forgave Durvasa and called off the spinning chakra, saving Durvasa's life. In the end, the mystical powers of Durvasa proved to be less powerful than the devotional path of yoga that King Ambarish had been following.

## ～つ The Power of Love

There is no shortage of stories in the yoga scriptures that warn us about the misuse of yogic powers. In one story, the Buddha came across a yogi who, after many years of penance and practice, developed the ability to walk on water. The Buddha smiled and said to the yogi, "I can let myself be rowed across the river for a few pennies. What is the use spending so many years on attaining mystical powers?"

Perhaps we have to ask ourselves, what kind of perfection or power do we actually want to attain by our practice of yoga? The siddhis may be attractive to some, but if one doesn't take care, they are likely to reinforce the ego and easily distract one from the higher goal of yoga, which is to transcend the ego altogether.

The true benefit of siddhasana is its ability to give us the space to meditate on the power and beauty of selfless giving and unconditional love. Love is a weakness so strong that it cannot be broken, and it is therefore the greatest power imaginable. Krishna, as the embodiment of the Divine, says in the Bhagavad Gita to his friend Arjuna, "Be mindful of me. With love offer selflessly to me, sacrifice willingly for me, act out of reverence for me. In this way you shall come to me, this I promise you, for you are dearly loved by me." Cultivating this understanding and trying to live our lives in a spirit of giving accordingly is the true power, or siddhi, of this meditative pose.

# dhanurasana

## BOW POSE

*Dhanurasana* means "bow pose." In this pose the body is bent backwards like an archer's bow, with the torso and legs representing the body of the bow and the arms, the string. In addition to providing the general benefits of a backbend, such as creating openness in the upper spine and heart, this pose improves shoulder flexibility.

## Finding the Right Effort

In dhanurasana the challenge is to find the right amount of extension in the pose. On a real bow, if the tension on the string is too great, it will break. And if there isn't enough tension, the string will not have enough force to launch the arrow. The same principle applies for stringed instruments. To get the right tone, a musician must put the string under the right amount of tension. Finding our balance under just enough intensity, or bodily stress, in a pose is one of the key challenges in asana. This principle may also be applied to situations in our daily lives. The question is, how do we determine the right amount of effort when we're in challenging situations?

## Arjuna's Dilemma

The great archer Arjuna once faced a terrible choice. War was imminent, and he knew that if he joined the battle, he would have to fight his own kinsmen. So he asked his friend and guide Krishna for counsel. Arjuna's dilemma is immortalized in the great yogic scripture the Bhagavad Gita, or the "Song of Divinity," divided into eighteen chapters that each cover a different aspect of yoga philosophy, and which has since become one of the most sacred and beloved texts on yoga. This text, which is contained within the larger Indian epic Mahabharata, is a dialogue between Arjuna, who represents our ego, and Krishna, who represents our higher consciousness. The text is a spiritual discourse that conveys practical yogic wisdom.

The Gita opens with Arjuna and Krishna standing on their chariot, overlooking the assembled armies. The approaching war is the last chance to reclaim a kingdom that was unjustly stolen from Arjuna and his brothers many years before. Faced with the

45

prospect of having to fight and probably kill his own relatives and former teachers, Arjuna falters and lets his bow slip from his hands. He then puts his dilemma before Krishna, who functions as both his mentor and charioteer. What follows is a conversation captured in seven hundred Sanskrit verses.

Krishna starts by telling Arjuna he needs to fulfill his duty (known as *dharma*) as a warrior by fighting for a just cause against evil. Krishna then proceeds to teach Arjuna about the science of the soul, or yoga. He tells Arjuna that he need not worry about the deaths that will occur during the war, because no one in the world can kill the immortal soul. Fire cannot burn it and water cannot drown it. When the body is slain, the soul passes on to another body, just as we exchange old garments for a new set of clothes.

Krishna also advises Arjuna to accept both happiness and distress with detachment, because they come and go like the seasons and are merely sensory impressions. Many more profound teachings about and insights into the working of the mind and the forces of nature follow. The Gita ends with Krishna advising Arjuna to surrender himself to him, because Krishna is the personification of the Divine. This surrender is filled with love and support, and not at all like raising a white flag and giving up.

The teachings of the Gita are so vivid because Arjuna, with all of his doubt, is all too human. Life often presents difficult challenges, which sometimes make us want to give up rather than take appropriate action. In a sense we are all warriors, having to fight our way to enlightenment.

What the Bhagavad Gita does above all is place our life in a much larger context. Instead of being reactive when difficulties challenge our ego, we can learn, with the help of the Gita, to identify the ego and transcend it. We can start to look at obstacles in life as opportunities for personal growth, because we understand that there is a grand plan, of which each of us is a small yet essential part. The challenging bow pose creates an opportunity to apply the advice of the Gita in our asana practice: We try to strike that perfect balance of being fearless, taking responsibility for our life, and not giving in to difficulties, while at the same time staying detached from the results of our actions.

# balasana

## CHILD'S POSE

*Balasana* is the pose of the child (*bala*), in which
the body is draped over folded legs, representing
a child in the womb. It is a resting pose that is often
performed after a challenging asana or when we
need some time to let our mind and body absorb
the practice. When we are in an innocent and
receptive state of mind, it is easiest to be
transformed by our yoga practice.

❋

## The Childhood Play of Krishna

Although Krishna is known mostly for his role in the Bhagavad Gita, stories about his childhood involve enjoyable insights. After his miraculous birth at which all the signs of his divinity were present, Krishna grew up in the idyllic surroundings of the forests of Vrindavan. Once, when Krishna and his brother Balaram were playing in the courtyard, Krishna took a scoop of earth in his hand and ate it. When Balaram saw this, he ran to their mother, Yashoda, and told her, "Mother, Krishna is eating dirt. He may choke on it!" Unsurprised at yet another of her son's naughty tricks, Yashoda grabbed hold of Krishna and questioned him.

"Have you eaten mud?" she demanded. Although Krishna's face was covered with mud, he replied, "Oh no, Mother. Balaram is lying. I haven't touched any mud." Of course Yashoda didn't believe him, and she made Krishna open his mouth. When Yashoda looked inside, she didn't see any mud. Instead she saw the whole universe and all the galaxies.

Although Krishna's parents and friends were vaguely aware of his divinity, his childish charm as a toddler made them forget. This play of forgetfulness of divinity is called *lila*. It facilitates the highest type of connection a soul can have in relation to the Divine. This forgetfulness allows Krishna's friends to play and joke with him in a way that would not be possible if they were aware of (and potentially intimidated by) his divinity. In a similar way, a president of a country also needs to forget his official function when he is playing horse with his grandson riding on his back. This is one of the paradoxes in yoga philosophy: First we need to remember our divine nature, and when we are established in it we need to forget it again in order to stay engaged in the world. This is however a playful type of forgetfulness in which we do not loose connection with our soul. When Yashoda looked into Krishna's mouth, she saw

the whole of creation contained within it. Everything is in God, and God is in everything. There is no duality here, just play for the sake of play.

## ~⤴ Transcending the Ego through Surrender

Often children are the best teachers. It is said that Yoga is actually very easy and very difficult at the same time. It is simple because the only thing we need to do is stop clinging to our ego. But that is also one of the hardest things we can do, given the subtle workings of the ego, which we continually reinforce.

According to both the Yoga Sutra and the Bhagavad Gita, the ultimate goal of yoga lies in our surrender to a higher power. Yoga is usually regarded as a practice that liberates us from the ego, but at the same time it binds us to the Divine through love. And this is what the child's pose symbolizes. It is the childlike surrender to the Divine that opens up the pathways of grace. And all past, present, and future sages of yoga will testify that grace is what we need, as we are all dependent on something that is greater than ourselves. We often do not realize this enough, and take many things for granted—the ground we stand on, the air we breathe. But it may all be taken away from us at any moment in time. And then surrender is all that is left to us. In surrender we truly open ourselves up to receive, and also to give. Balasana invites us to cultivate this childlike quality.

# dandasana

## STAFF POSE

*Danda* means "rod" or "staff." In the seated version of *dandasana*, the legs are straight and the torso is upright. In *chaturanga* (four-limbed) dandasana, the body is straight like a stick and parallel to the floor, with only hands and feet touching it.

## ⌒ Krishna Supports Mount Govardhan

Once the cow herders of Vrindavan, led by Krishna's father, Nanda, decided to perform a ritual to honor Indra. As the ruler of the heavens, it is Indra who sends the clouds. They reasoned that without the clouds there is no rain and no grain and therefore no food for the cattle.

Krishna protested to his father, Nanda, "We are not farmers or traders. We are cow herders and live in the forests. Our gods should be the cattle and the mountains. Let's forget about Indra and worship Mount Govardhan instead. That is our proper *dharma, our spiritual duty.*" Nanda and the other cow herders agreed and they turned their worship to the mountain with many offerings of food.

Indra was very angry that people had stopped worshipping him. He summoned his favorite clouds and instructed them to inundate Mount Govardhan with torrents of rain and assault it with strong winds. To protect the cow herders and the cows from the flooding, Krishna uprooted Govardhan and held it aloft like an umbrella. The entire mountain was balanced on one of Krishna's pinky fingers, as if it were a staff. The cow herders and the cattle took refuge underneath. The people of Vrindavan were amazed and tried to help Krishna by putting their own sticks and canes against the mountain as well.

For seven nights Indra poured rain on the mountain, but not one drop touched Krishna or any of his fellow cow herders. Indra admired this divine display so much that after the seventh night of rain, he ceased his tumult. Indra eventually befriended and honored Krishna by bathing him with the help of his elephant.

## ～つ The Guru Principle

In addition to symbolizing support, the danda or stick also represents the recognition of a good teacher. The danda has been likened to the prostrate position with which a pupil paid respect to a teacher in yogic culture. The yoga tradition has always placed a lot of emphasis on the importance of a teacher who can help us to apply the teachings of this tradition to our life.

## ～つ The Story of Bilvamangala

There once lived a man named Bilvamangala. He lusted madly for a prostitute called Chintamani, and visited her daily. One night there was a terrible storm raging over the village where he lived. But Bilvamangala was so crazy for Chintamani that he decided to visit her anyway. In order to do so he had to cross a river, which had swollen and was moving dangerously fast because of the heavy rains. Bilvamangala couldn't be deterred and decided to swim across. When he was halfway across the river he was so exhausted that he nearly drowned, but he saved his life by grabbing hold of a wooden log. After he reached the other shore he realized that the log of wood was actually a corpse.

When Bilvamangala reached Chintamani's house, the storm made so much noise that she didn't hear him knocking on the door. Bilvamangala decided to climb onto the balcony by pulling himself up with the help of a rope that was dangling from it. Because of his blinding lust, he didn't notice that the rope was actually a cobra, which bit him. Bilvamangala tumbled down, and the resulting hubbub awakened Chintamani, who finally opened the door.

When Chintamani saw the deplorable state of Bilvamangala she scolded him. "You have so much desire for this bag of blood and bones that is my body. If you even would have had a little bit of that desire to realize divinity, you would have achieved self realization long ago."

Bilvamangala suddenly realized his foolishness and accepted Chintamani as his first guru. He swore to never be deluded by his vision any longer and took out his own eyes.

The story of Bilvamangala shows us the deeper meaning behind the guru principle which states that the guru is operating within us and in all the beings around us at all times. The person who inspires us on our path to self-realization can come to us in any shape or form. He may be our neighbor next door, or even our own child, as we will see in the case of Prahlad in the story about simhasana on page 100.

There is a  spiritual poem called the "Uddhava Gita," in which the guru principle is wonderfully explained by a wandering saint. He relates that all he knows he has learned from his gurus, including the mountain, the sky, the spider, water, fire, the sea, children, serpents, and many more. From a tree he has learned to dedicate himself to others, and from his own body he has learned that matter is always changing.

Yoga is largely practiced through our relationships with others. It is about coming out of the cocoon of the ego to share the love that we have with our friends and family and all with whom we come in contact. It is also about gratitude for having received this wonderful practice and philosophy, which can help us transform our lives in ways we may never have dreamed. The gratitude we cultivate through our practice and begin to feel toward the tradition, its teachers, and practitioners is only natural. The surrender of our ego to all of our teachers is mirrored in dandasana, and reminds us of this gratitude.

# poses of the gods

Natarajasana

Virasana

Virabhadrasana

Halasana

Hanumanasana

Kurmasana

Anjaneyasana

Garudasana

Simhasana

SINCE YOGA WAS BORN in the context of the spiritual culture of ancient India, we can enhance our practice by becoming familiar with the world of gods and goddesses that is connected with it. Their stories contain archetypes that speak to our nature, tendencies, troubles, and joys. For example, *hanumanasana* is more meaningful if we know something of the character of Hanuman. The physical postures of the asanas contain within them the essence of the mythology that they represent.

Each asana carries the potential to help us more fully understand the Divine and create a personal relationship to it. Yoga doesn't tell us to believe in a particular form of religion or worship in a prescribed way, but it does ask us to recognize and honor a higher power that is beyond our small selves. In order to help us find a means of connecting with it in a personal way, yoga calls this personal form of divinity *Isvara*.

In the Yoga Sutra, Patanjali recommends that we surrender ourselves to Isvara. It is the only recommendation that is repeated four times throughout the text. It reads, "Isvara pranidhanad va," which means, "When we dedicate ourselves to the divine, we become divine." Or at least we are more able to recognize that bit of the Divine source that resides within us. Isvara is a personal form of God we can relate to. What is most important here is that we find some common ground with something that would otherwise seem too grand and unattainable. Isvara brings God out of the ether and into our hearts and bodies. As we express these divine asanas, we are giving ourselves the opportunity to relate to that divine element within.

If we start looking at the asanas from this perspective, our yoga practice can only become richer. And who knows? What seems otherworldly at first may even become a new world in which we can feel quite at home.

# natarajasana

## LORD OF THE DANCE POSE

*Natarajasana* is a standing balance posture that involves bending one knee and grasping the ankle or foot from behind. As the yogi then leans forward and kicks back with the foot, an arm stretches forward to complete the pose. This pose is the physical embodiment of one of the many guises of Shiva.

## ⌒ The King of the Dance

Nietzsche once wrote, "If they want me to believe in their god, they'll have to sing better songs. . . . I could only believe in a god who dances." As one of the Hindu trinity, Shiva has many different personae that illuminate his essence. The most well known is his role as the King Dancer, or in Sanskrit, Nataraja. In this guise he is commonly portrayed with snakes around his neck, dreadlocks standing on end, balancing atop a tiny dwarf, and encircled by a ring of fire. Oddly enough, this imposing image conveys a lot of compassion if we know how to look at it through a yogic lens.

The ages of the world are long, and at the end of each one, Shiva stands ready to turn it all to dust, so that yet another world can be created to exist for yet another age. While we, as mere mortals, will never live long enough to see an entire age from the beginning to the end, the deathless form of Shiva as Nataraja sees each age as only a passing moment in time. In one of his hands he holds a drum, and with each beat he signals the death and rebirth of another age. And this drum beats fast. Undaunted by the slow pace of cosmic disintegration, Shiva dances to his own music within a circle of flame known as *samsara*.

Samsara is the cyclical pattern in which we are all stuck—the constant repetition of birth, life, and death. This corresponds well to the idea of reincarnation. Another way to think of samsara is as the many ways in which we get stuck in patterns and habits throughout our lives that don't serve us, but rather inhibit us. This spinning karmic cycle of samsara does not trouble Shiva. He just sees it as one more rhythm to dance to. Shiva is unafraid of this binding wheel of fire, just as he is unafraid of the serpents around his neck.

Snakes are potent metaphors within yogic philosophy, and for most of us they are frightening creatures—especially the cobra that dangles from Shiva's neck as he dances. The poison the cobra carries symbolizes the toxic nature of *avidya*, the misunderstanding of ourselves as something other than divine. The cobra's poison is not toxic to our lord of the dance. He has found the remedy to that affliction, which is enlightened knowledge, and he carries its symbolic flame in one of his palms. Yoga seeks to rid us of the ignorance of avidya through various practices, such as asana, pranayama, and meditation, and by constantly reminding us of the fact that we are all divine in nature. Still we constantly forget, become locked into the cycle of samsara, and fall prey to the poison of avidya.

In the depiction of Shiva as the King Dancer, ignorance is represented by the tiny dwarf-like demon upon which he stands. This seemingly helpless creature is usually busy causing mischief, which mainly consists of keeping us all caught up in our own daily dramas. Once again, Shiva proves to be the master. He does not let this little character get the best of him and instead uses him as a pedestal for his dance. By standing over the demon of ignorance, he is able to have a higher gaze, or a higher level of consciousness, which allows him to rise above daily drama. For him, the only thing worth paying attention to is the rhythm of the dance.

Shiva, the cosmic dancer, is not filled with guilt over the destruction of each age. He knows that everything that is born must also die. He understands that destruction clears the path for rebirth and that in rebirth and growth there is compassion. Brahma the creator cannot do his work properly if Shiva the destroyer has not done his. It is Shiva's destruction that provides the fertile platform for Brahma's process of rebuilding.

## Dissolving Fear & Embracing Change

In order to dance like Shiva, we must feel free. Freedom comes from knowing there is nothing that binds us permanently. Shiva's dance is born out of a liberation from the fear of change. He teaches us to ride

the wave of change as if we're on a cosmic surfboard, coasting toward the shore of bliss. Shiva's lessons are integral to the yogic path.

In the Yoga Sutra, Patanjali outlines five obstacles that prevent us from true freedom, which are called the *kleshas*. The first is avidya, and the fifth and most powerful obstacle is the fear of death, or *abhinivesha*. Death is the ultimate change and takes many forms in our lives, until the greatest death of all, which comes at the end. As the lord of death and destruction, Shiva understands that change, even one as great as death, is really the only constant in the universe.

The fear of change causes more stress than possibly any other fear. It is fear of changing borders that causes many wars. And the fear of changing our views makes us cling to dogma. The sheer desire to have things remain the same, according to the Buddha, is the nature of suffering. Conversely, embracing change liberates us from suffering.

The scientific law of conservation of mass states that matter can neither be created nor destroyed. In essence, if you want to make something new, you must destroy something old or allow it to die. So Shiva, in his ultimate wisdom, is utterly compassionate in his destruction. He gives us the freedom to demolish our social norms and create something entirely new. He creates the space for us to make positive, abundant choices in our lives and let go of fear. If we truly want change, then we must learn to embrace a little death and destruction.

Natarajasana allows us to experience a couple of physical elements that can bring about fear in our bodies. Backbending and balancing both elicit fear because of the openness and bravery they require. We tend to store fear in our heart (according to the chakra system), and when we open the heart, we give ourselves an opportunity to let go of fear. Likewise, balancing gives us an opportunity to overcome our natural fear of falling and to be brave and free. If we can backbend and balance with the same sense of liberation with which Nataraja dances, then it will be easier for us to embrace this freedom in our minds and hearts.

# virabhadrasana

## WARRIOR POSES

The series of warrior poses includes three variations
that could easily be considered the most iconic
of the standing postures. All three are strong
standing poses. The first is oriented toward the
front, with arms up overhead; the second is
oriented to the side, with arms outstretched; and
the third is again oriented to the front, but with
arms stretched forward, and the body balanced on
one leg. Although the three postures are generally
not taught in succession, they all fit together and
illustrate the power and ferocity of the warrior.

## ⌒ Dreadlocked & Destructive

The great Shiva has a fierce and unending love for his consort, Shakti. Shakti has many incarnations, as the gods often do, and in her various forms she is known by different names. During one of her many lifetimes, she was known as Sati and was born to a mortal father named Daksha. Sati was incredibly beautiful and wholly devoted to Shiva. He was her secret love, and she kept this hidden within the depths of her heart while she was growing up, worshipping him and professing her love to him only in private.

Daksha wasn't a huge fan of Shiva. His ideal mate for his daughter didn't include a dreadlocked guy covered in ash who was known to have a bad temper and sat in meditation for thousands of years on top of a remote mountain. Not to mention his choice of clothing, which was pretty scant. Nonetheless, Sati's heart was set upon Shiva, and she would never be happy unless they could be together.

When Sati came of age, her father had a grand party to which he invited every eligible suitor in the land—except, of course, Shiva. Well, being a clever young woman, Sati knew just how to work around her father and get what she wanted. During the party, she mixed and mingled with the other partygoers, making her father proud by feigning interest in a few of the young men. However, when the time came to choose her partner, she threw the garland she had been wearing around her neck up in the air and invoked the name of the great Shiva. He then appeared in the sky, donned the garland, and fell to Sati's side with great joy. According to tradition, whoever wore the garland must be the one to wed the available daughter, so Daksha had no choice but to give his lovely princess to the god he despised so much.

Daksha's fury would not go unavenged. After Sati and Shiva were wed and living happily on the mountaintop, Daksha threw yet another grand soiree, and again he made a point not to invite Shiva, which was an insult of the highest order. Sati became very upset that her father still would not accept the choice that made her so happy.

During the jubilee, Sati appeared before her father with a saddened face and sorrow in her heart. All the guests turned to see Daksha's beautiful daughter standing and weeping before him. Daksha, who loved his daughter very much, was distraught to see her so upset but stood by his decision to continue to reject Shiva as her partner. Sati's fury and great sadness ignited a fire that burned so brightly inside her that she went up in flames right in the middle of the party and was reduced to a pile of ashes before her father's very eyes.

Sati's self-immolation caused a great disturbance in the universe, which Shiva felt in his meditative state upon Mount Kailash. He knew instantly that something had happened to his beloved. When the heavenly minstrel Narada came to him with the tale of what had occurred, Shiva became absolutely furious. In his fury and rage, he stood on top of the mountain, ripped a dreadlock from his head, and threw it on the ground. With the force of his anger, this dreadlock snaked into the earth and all the way down through the mountain, only to emerge in the center of the party, right in the very spot where Sati's ashes lay.

The dreadlock was transformed into Virabhadra, the great warrior, who rose out of the ground (think warrior 1 pose, palms together, face upturned), drew his sword (think warrior 2, arms open), and sliced off Daksha's head. When it fell to the ground, Virabhadra bent to pick it up and reached forward to place it upon a stake (think warrior 3, arms reaching forward). This shocking act caused quite an uproar among the partygoers, who tried to flee the scene because they feared for their own heads.

In the world of the gods things can happen almost instantaneously, and this dire situation required the great Sati to secure another form very quickly so she could go reason with Shiva. She donned a new body and showed up at the party again, but this time, she scolded Shiva for beheading her father. "Look at what you've done!" she exclaimed to Virabhadra, knowing that Shiva would hear her on the mountaintop. "I know my father didn't do a kind thing, but it wasn't your place to step into the middle of it and kill him. Do you really think that is going to solve our problem and make him accept you?"

Shiva hadn't really thought of that. He was just so angry at Daksha, he didn't really consider how Sati would feel or that it would start a dramatic chain of events that would actually make things worse, not better. The problem was, he hadn't thought at all.

Sati demanded, "Make this right, right now! I don't care how you do it, just fix it." Well, Shiva himself arrived at the party, where a few lone partygoers were peering from behind trees to see what the great would do. He came marching in with his trident in hand and waved Virabhadra aside to keep him at bay. Shiva looked around and realized immediately that Daksha's head was not suitable for reattachment, so he found the nearest replacement, which happened to be a goat. Off came the head of the goat, and onto Daksha's body it went. Shiva breathed a great exhale, and life returned to Daksha's body. The object of his rage was standing in front of him, but Daksha suddenly felt grateful that Shiva had realized the error of his ways and made amends.

In his gratitude, and with the realization that he had not behaved in a dignified way toward Shiva, Daksha held one final party and made Shiva and Sati his guests of honor.

## ᴖ a Warrior's Code of Behavior

Topics of conversation among yogis are often lighthearted, but the reality is that life isn't always just butterflies and rainbows. It gets hard, and tough decisions need to be made. Challenges arise that shake us to our very core, as was the case for Shiva when he was faced with his beloved's death at, he believed, the hands of her father. The knee-jerk reaction most of us experience is exactly that—a reaction. Often our impulses, like Shiva's, lead us to seek revenge. We may not always act on that impulse, as Shiva did, but we may secretly want to, turning such thoughts over and over in our head.

The truth is, things rarely go as planned. For example, how much time have we spent in our mind playing out an entire argument? We think, "Okay, if he says this, then I'll respond that way. Then, he'll probably say that, so I'll say this back." In the end, the conversation rarely goes the way we want it to. We deal with disappointments and failed expectations every single day. This kind of constant stress can lead an aspiring yogi to wonder, how can we resist the impulse of a heated moment? How can we bring that bliss and simplicity we experience on our mat to the daily challenges of our lives? There is a profound aphorism in the Yoga Sutra that gives us the perfect prescription:

> *Maitri karuna muditopekshanam sukha dukha punya apunya visayanam bhavanatash chitta prasadanam. (YS 1.33)*

> "In order to preserve an elevated state of mind, be happy for those who are happy, cultivate compassion for those who are sad, feel delight for those deemed to be lucky [virtuous or righteous], and experience indifference toward those perceived to be wicked."

Although it seems easy to be happy for those who are happy, in reality it's not. Daksha could not be happy for his daughter, despite the fact that she had finally joined with the love that she had so long desired. Likewise, some of her potential suitors may have had a hard time feeling delighted about her good fortune in landing Shiva as a mate (little did they know that she'd been praying for him for years!).

Behaving with compassion or detachment isn't easy either. When Sati came to Daksha in sadness because of his rejection of Shiva, he could not feel compassion for her, because he was too caught up in being right. Shiva, on the other hand, looked upon Daksha's unkindness toward his daughter as wicked. Instead of remaining indifferent, he sought revenge and sent Virabhadra to exact it.

Even the gods seem to screw up sometimes, although their apparent mistakes are really made to teach us valuable lessons. They give hope to the rest of us yogis, who try hard every day to maintain a yogi's state of mind. Having a sweet or uplifted outlook, which Patanjali refers to as chitta prasadanam, is really the optimal state in which to pursue a yoga practice.

We begin doing a posture in a certain way, but we continually deepen our experience of the posture in order to further our practice. It's the same when we take our practice off the mat and become yoga warriors out in the world. Patanjali's Yoga Sutra gives us the tools of happiness, compassion, delight, and indifference. He asks us to use them to preserve our elevated state of mind. Yoga practice really begins when things get hard—in life or on the mat.

It is not easy being a warrior, especially one who is constantly fighting against a reactive mind. Possibly the greatest lesson we can learn from Shiva and Virabhadra is that when we err, we always have the opportunity to step forward and do our best to make things right. Warrior poses are a reminder that ferocity exists not only to destroy but also to allow us sufficient strength to achieve integrity, compassion, and a loving state of mind.

# hanumanasana, anjaneyasana & virasana

MONKEY POSE
LOW LUNGE
HERO POSE

These three poses are grouped together because they all illustrate the story of the beloved monkey god Hanuman. *Hanumanasana*, the pose that bears his name, is a full split, facing forward. *Anjaneyasana* is a deep, kneeling lunge, and *virasana* is a seated pose designed to stretch the thighs and create healthy knee joints.

All three poses stretch the psoas muscle, which runs from the middle of the spine to the inner thigh. This muscle gets a particularly intense stretch in virasana when one reclines. This very deep core muscle initiates all of our movements, and it is pivotal in the fight-or-flight response that is built into our bodies. For many people, the fight-or-flight response is almost continuously stimulated by a low-grade application of stress, which is so much a part of Western lifestyles, and results in a chronically locked psoas. The effects of stress are augmented by our daily habit of sitting for long periods of time on chairs, which also shortens and tightens this long, rope-like muscle.

Because of its relation to the fight-or-flight response, which typically engages when we are fearful, the psoas is where we generally hide fear. The process of opening the psoas and encouraging its release through these three related poses gives us an opportunity to physically shed our fears and move into a state of fearlessness. And that state is exactly what Hanuman embodies.

## Fearless Monkey

Anjana was a beautiful woman who deeply desired to become a mother, so she prayed daily for the miracle of a child. The wind god Vayu admired Anjana very much, and when he heard her prayer, he decided to help her out. He blessed a few grains of rice and sent them with his bird friends, who were flying her way. Anjana was engaged in her daily prayer ritual. She had her arms stretched upward in anjali mudra, ready to receive the grace of God, when she received a few grains of rice instead. She knew better than to question what came to her through prayer, so she opened her mouth and tossed in the rice. Upon her consumption of the blessed rice, she became pregnant.

When her baby Anjaneya (which meant "son of Anjana") was born, he was quite a precocious youngster. He was half mortal and half divine, since Vayu was his father. His demigod status is what often led him into big trouble. One morning Anjaneya woke up and saw what he thought was a giant mango floating in the sky. Since mangoes were his favorite treat, he immediately leapt up into the sky and rushed toward the fruit, not realizing it was actually the sun. When the sun god Surya saw this little troublemaker racing to take a big bite out of him, he threw a lightning bolt, which hit the boy in the jaw, killing him instantly and sending him tumbling to the ground.

When Vayu learned what Surya had done, his great fury made him take a deep breath. It was so deep that he sucked up all the air from the earth, and all the beings began to suffocate. The gods called an emergency meeting to try and placate both Vayu and Surya and restore order. Vayu refused to exhale until he got his son, Anjaneya, back. But Surya didn't want this potentially dangerous child running around unrestrained.

Finally, an agreement was reached. Anjaneya would be renamed Hanuman, which referred to the broken jaw he received from the lightning bolt (*hanuh* means "jaw" in Sanskrit). He would be revived, but cursed with short-term memory so that he would never recall his godliness long enough to cause any real harm. If he believed himself to be just a mortal, what damage could he possibly do?

And finally, he would be removed from his mother's care so that he could start a new life. The trusted monkey king, Sugriva, agreed to take Hanuman under his wing, and the little boy took the shape of a monkey to better match his new family.

## a Monkey's Best Friend

Hanuman grew to be an invaluable asset to the proud warriors of the monkey clan. One day as he was wandering through the forest, he met King Ram. The connection between the two was instantaneous. Hanuman immediately swore to never leave Ram's side, and Ram trusted him implicitly. The two were inseparable, as close as peas in a pod.

Ram had a wife named Sita, who was known for her beauty and heavenly qualities. It wasn't long before the evil demon Ravana grew uncontrollably jealous of the couple. His envy blinded his good judgment, and he went to war to take over Ram's kingdom and kidnapped Sita for himself, taking her to his island kingdom of Lanka. Ram had to lead his troops into battle to protect his land, so he couldn't go save the lovely Sita. In his place he sent his good friend Hanuman to rescue her.

Hanuman took off for the tip of the subcontinent with no idea how he would accomplish his task, but he knew he must do it. His sheer love for his best friend helped him overcome any doubts he had about his own abilities. When Hanuman reached the coast and looked out over the great, vast ocean toward the island of Lanka, he knelt down in prayer. The pose he knelt in, with one knee up and one knee folded under, inspired the original virasana. He closed his eyes and prayed to be filled with the grace it would take to do the impossible. During his prayer, his unwavering faith never faltered. When he felt as if he had summoned enough energy, he pressed his feet firmly into the ground with such force that it caused a shock wave to ripple through the land, flattening the trees and hills behind him. He was propelled into the air and soared toward Lanka over the open sea.

## The Faithful Hero

It is important to remember that when Hanuman knelt down to pray for the grace to accomplish the impossible, he was already capable of achieving his goal. As the son of the wind, Hanuman could do anything. He could grow very large or very small, move mountains, and even change his shape all together. But he was constantly forgetting his divinity, and so he turned to his faith—which in Sanskrit we call *shraddha*—to give him the confidence to do what he knew he must accomplish. Many of us shrink before impossible tasks, or even tasks that are just a bit hard, because we are just like Hanuman. We easily forget that there is a part of us that is also divine and can accomplish the impossible. And we forget about the element of shraddha, which is ingrained in every human heart, just as it was within Hanuman's.

Throughout human history, there has always been some form of prayer to give human beings the space and time to grow that element of faith within their hearts. It is with faith and hope that we can go forth with confidence and leap across oceans, change the world, or simply fall back in love.

## Soaring to New Heights

As he flew over the ocean toward his destiny, one of Hanuman's feet reached forward and one foot reached back, like the famous split pose, *hanumanasana*, that yogis know today. Despite encountering numerous obstacles, including a demon that rose from the water to try and gobble him up, Hanuman landed confidently on the island of Lanka. He searched until he discovered Sita in the gardens of Ravana's palace and transformed himself into a cat in order to

sneak in and let her know that Ram would be coming to save her. She gave him her hairpin to let Ram know that he'd found her, and Hanuman gave Sita Ram's ring as a promise of her future rescue. And rescue her they did. Eventually Ram brought the war to Ravana's doorstep, and with Hanuman's help, Ravana was defeated and Sita was saved.

When balance and peace were restored to the land, Ram held a great gathering back at his palace and asked Hanuman to be his guest of honor. Hanuman was called up to be awarded, and Ram presented him with his very own precious gem–encrusted gold bracelet. The audience gasped in awe and pride at this divine exchange, but Hanuman gazed curiously at the bangle. He knocked on it and chewed it with his teeth. When some gems popped off, he used them to try and peer more closely at the gold, but looked dissatisfied at what he didn't find. Ram, Sita, and the onlookers were shocked at Hanuman's seeming ungratefulness. Ram asked Hanuman why he was so unhappy with his gift.

Hanuman looked at Ram and explained, "Ram, every moment I chant your name. I chant your name so I can constantly remember how much I love you. I chant your name so much that even the fibers of my heart have your name written upon them. This bracelet is worth nothing to me if it does not bear your name. Here, let me show you." It was then that Hanuman knelt down in front of Ram and Sita, dug his fingers into his chest, and opened it up to reveal the contents of his heart. Inside were Ram and Sita, perfect and complete, and on every fiber of Hanuman's heart was written Ram's name. With each "thump-thump," the chant "Ram, Ram" quietly sounded.

## ∼◡ The Constant One

Hanuman's journey, as recounted in the Ramayana (the epic tale of Ram), is one of faith, fearlessness, and complete devotion. Hanuman is said to embody all of the qualities of the yogi, and his story reflects our own in many ways. How many times have we forgotten our own divinity only to fall back into the same self-defeating way of thinking over and over? Who hasn't had a crisis of faith and wondered if some burden wasn't too great to bear, or whether some task wasn't impossible to complete? Hanuman teaches us that there is one thing that allows us to override all of our doubts and fears. That one thing is love.

The tradition of bhakti yoga is focused on cultivating this attitude so perfectly that all our fears and doubts fall away, and we are left only with the remembrance of our true self. The tool of the bhakti yogi is the repetition of a *mantra*, or a short phrase, which focuses one's attention on an object of devotion. For Hanuman, the object of devotion was Ram, so he chanted his name repeatedly. His poor memory meant that he would often forget his task, or associations, but he always remembered his best friend. And so he began and ended every sentence with Ram's name. Every spare moment he had, he chanted it. Eventually, every fiber of his being pulsed with Ram's name, and that perfect attention caused his soul to merge with the object of his devotion to embody love itself, which is why Ram and Sita reside inside his heart.

Many yoga practitioners are discovering the power of chant to call up deep and joyful emotions. Whether simply listening to chant music or participating in *kirtans* (call-and-response style singing), it is easy for practitioners to feel the effects of that simple repetition. These exercises are related to the deeper experience of mantra recitation, which many yogis use during their meditation. Mantras can be repeated out loud, sung as part of a song, or repeated silently to oneself. They are designed to liberate us from the fear and illusion that keep us small, allowing us to manifest our fully realized potential. The word "mantra" is derived from *manas* ("mind") and *trava* ("liberate"), meaning "that which liberates the mind." The key factor to success in yoga is the consistency of the repetition. When the practice is constant, the coming is inevitable. And what comes, as Hanuman found, is the undeniable presence of complete compassion and the melting of fear.

## ～ The Hero Inside

Each of Hanuman's poses embodies the fearlessness, bravery, strength, friendship, and compassion that he so clearly expressed through each of his adventures. *Vira*, the root word of "virasana," is Sanskrit for "hero." One way to embody that word is to be full of faith. It is said that the difference between the hero and the coward is that the hero acts. When fear stops most, the hero, filled with faith, pursues the seemingly impossible, knowing that it is the only way to soar to new heights. Fear can keep us small or challenge us to rise above the meekness. The poet Andrea Gibson writes, "I don't believe in miracles, because miracles are the impossible coming true, and everything is possible." It is this kind of possibility that infuses each of the poses dedicated to Hanuman. Each addresses, in some way, our power to overcome fear and gives us an opportunity to create space for the impossibilities in our lives.

# halasana

## PLOW POSE

*Halasana* means "plow pose" and refers to a plow that tills the dead earth to bring forth life. In plow pose, the practitioner lies on the floor, lifts the legs up and over the head, placing the toes on the floor behind the head. Halasana stretches the spine and stimulates the abdominal organs and the thyroid gland. It also balances the throat chakra.

## ⟍⟋ The Story of Haladhara

Krishna's older brother, Balarama, was also known as Haladhara because he carried (*dhara*) a plow (*hala*). Despite their quarrels and differences, Haladhara helped Krishna to overcome many demons in the forests of Vrindavan while they were growing up, and the two maintained a great relationship throughout their lives.

One lovely afternoon, Haladhara decided that he wanted to bathe in the great Yamuna River. Intoxicated by his favorite honey drink, he ordered the river to come close. Used to getting his way, Haladhara was surprised when the Yamuna River would not make its way over to him so that he could enjoy his bath. Rather than just walking over to the river, he took his great plow and dredged the river until it ran toward him.

## ⟍⟋ The Function of the Plow

According to yoga philosophy, all of our actions and thoughts leave traces in our consciousness. Our actions in this world can either remove impressions from the landscape of our consciousness or carve new ones. Just as Haladhara dragged the Yamuna to him with his plow, the yogi seeks to draw the mind back from its negative wanderings in order to absorb the positive. There is a sutra in the fourth chapter of the Yoga Sutra that talks about this kind of "plowing of the mind":

> *Nimittam aprayojakam prakëtînâm varaña-bhedas*
> *tu tatah kasetrikavat (YS 4.3).*

Essentially, this sutra says, just as a farmer plows his field to introduce water to the field for irrigation, if we remove the obstacles

in our path toward yoga, we can lead our mind toward it. In this way, the plow of our mind leads us to liberation, based on the quality of our thoughts. The plow pose provides an excellent opportunity to plow the field of our mind with positive thinking.

# kurmasana

## TORTOISE POSE

*Kurmasana* means "tortoise pose." In this pose, the arms are stretched out on the side of the body, the legs are over the arms, and the chest and shoulders ideally rest on the floor, resembling a tortoise with its legs out. The next stage, *supta kurmasana*, resembles a tortoise that has withdrawn into its shell. The hands are brought behind the body and the ankles cross behind the head. Kurmasana lengthens the back muscles and helps to release tightness in the sacrum and lumbar region.

## ᨆ Kurmavatara

Legend has it that the demigods had been cursed after insulting a sage, and because of this curse, many of them were slain in a war against the demons. Although the demigods possessed mystical powers and could bring the dead back to life, the remaining demigods were unable to use these powers to revive their fallen comrades. They approached Brahma for help. Realizing this case was beyond him, Brahma took the demigods to Vishnu, who was lying on the serpent Ananta in the ocean of possibility.

Vishnu advised the demigods to make a truce with the demons. Together they could produce what both groups desired— *amrita*, the nectar of immortality—by churning the cosmic ocean. In order to complete this task, he recommended that they place the contents of the ocean on the great mountain Mandara and use it as a churning rod. They did as Vishnu suggested and used Vasuki, the king of serpents, as a rope to churn the ocean and create the sacred potion.

The demons pulled Vasuki's tail and the demigods pulled his head. As the ocean began to churn, the mountain started to sink into it. At that moment Vishnu appeared in his tortoise form, which was called Kurmavatar, and supported the mountain on his back. The churning continued, but instead of producing the nectar of immortality, a terrible poison emerged from the cosmic ocean. The demigods and demons then petitioned Shiva to rescue them, which he did by drinking the poison. Shiva was able to hold the poison in his throat and return the ocean to its original divine state, but the vile liquid turned his throat blue.

The churning produced many other celestial items, such as a precious jewel, nymphs, and a divine cow. At some point in time Lakshmi, the goddess of fortune and consort of Vishnu, came out of the ocean. Finally Dhanvantari, the doctor of the demigods, appeared with the pot of the nectar of immortality. The demons forgot about their truce with the demigods and snatched the pot away. Then Vishnu came on the scene disguised as a beautiful woman who enchanted both the demons and demigods. She said she would distribute the nectar evenly among the gods and demons. Intoxicated by her beauty, the demons and demigods readily agreed. She had them sit in two rows, but by the time she had finished feeding the demigods, the pot of nectar was empty.

The path of the yogi is to churn the body with the rope of the mind through repeated practice in order to reach a state of freedom and joy. During the process of purification, a lot of debris may surface before there is nectar. This is why the support of well-wishers, fellow yogis, and teachers is welcome, just as the tortoise supported the mountain. The tortoise pose is a reminder that asana practice endows us with the strength and mental vigor we need to face challenges in life.

## Withdrawing the Senses

There is another important yogic practice represented by the tortoise. A tortoise that withdraws its limbs inside its shell is a great metaphor for the yogi in the fifth step of Patanjali's eight-limbed path, called *pratyahara*. It is the stage at which we withdraw our senses from the objects that surround us so the undistracted mind can then focus itself on the object of meditation. This connection between the tortoise and meditation is referred to in a verse of the Yoga Sutra, where Patanjali suggests that meditation on the tortoise nadi, an energy channel found in the sternal notch of the throat, brings about steadiness (YS 3.32). In meditation we come in contact with the more subtle layers of our awareness, and we come closer to our essence. In order for this to happen, the mind must first quiet down.

Focusing our attention is important not only when we sit down for meditation, but also when we are engaged in asana practice. Where is our mind? When we pay attention to it, we will surely notice that it tries to escape the present moment all the time. So

we begin by withdrawing the senses from distracting objects, then focus the mind in concentration (*dharana*), after which meditation (*dhyana*) will follow as a natural result after prolonged practice.

To clarify the relationship between the mind and the senses, they are often compared to a carriage drawn by horses. In this metaphor, the horses are the senses, which are wild and need to be controlled and guided by the reins of the mind. On the carriage, the driver holding the reins represents the intelligence. On its own, the mind only registers the impulses of the senses; those impulses need to be directed by the intelligence. When the intelligence has the reins of the mind in check and the senses are held under control, the carriage of our body can take the passenger of our soul safely to its destination.

In a well-known verse from the Bhagavad Gita, Arjuna laments to Krishna (his chariot driver) that the mind seems more difficult to control than the wind, but Krishna assures him that through continuous practice, he will prevail. And here we can take inspiration from the tortoise again: slow but steady wins the race. Kurmasana represents the stability and steadiness upon which we build our yoga practice.

# garudasana

## EAGLE POSE

*Garudasana* is named after Vishnu's carrier
Garuda, a divine bird with the head, wings, talons,
and beak of an eagle and the body and limbs of
a man, which is why the pose is commonly referred
to as eagle pose. The practitioner begins by
standing in *tadasana*, a standing pose with the
feet together and the hands at the side of the
body, then bends the knees, brings one leg over
the other, and if possible, hooks the foot behind
the calf of the standing leg. The arm on the side
of the body of the lifted leg is then hooked under
the other arm. The benefits of garudasana include
strengthening and stretching the ankles and
calves and improving balance.

## ᙡ Garuda Carries the Nectar

Garuda emerged from a huge egg, appearing as radiant as a million suns. Frightened by his power, the gods begged him to reduce himself in size and energy.

One day Garuda's mother, Vinata, lost a bet with the snakes and was held captive as a slave in the underground serpent city of Patala. The serpents declared that they would not release Vinata unless Garuda brought a cup of amrita (the nectar of immortality) from its place high atop a celestial mountain. To get to the nectar, Garuda had to pass through three deadly obstacles.

The first obstacle was a ring of fire. Garuda gulped up the water from a few rivers and extinguished the fire, flying through it easily. The second obstacle was a circular door with a spiked metal ring that spun in its frame. Using his mystical powers, Garuda made himself very small and slipped right through. Finally, Garuda reached the third obstacle—two venomous serpents. Garuda created a cloud of dust by wildly flapping his wings, which blinded the snakes. Then he killed them with his powerful beak.

At last, Garuda was able to deliver the nectar of immortality to the snakes in the city of Patala in order to free his mother. But just as the serpents were about to consume the amrita, the chief demigod Indra and the other gods arrived to reclaim the stolen nectar. The serpents quickly licked a few drops of the amrita, which was so powerful that it split their tongues in two, which is why, as the legend goes, snakes have a bifurcated tongue. The serpents held their part of the bargain and released Garuda's mother, but only after she promised her son that she would never make such dangerous bets in the future.

## The Garuda in Us

In a sense, we are all a bit like Garuda. We are spiritual beings who are larger than life. Having been born in a material body, we have reduced ourselves in size and energy, and in this way, some of our vast spiritual potential remains hidden. The eagle pose starts with arms and legs open and extended, and then the body is reduced in size as we pull into ourselves. We hold the pose and then release, returning to openness. As spiritual beings living a human experience, we are constantly faced with obstacles that we overcome by turning to our divine nature, just as Garuda used his divine power to free his mother.

# simhasana

## LION POSE

*Simhasana*, or lion pose, is performed by sitting on the knees like a sphinx with the fingers outstretched. On the exhale, the practitioner sticks the tongue out and roars like a lion, while the eyes look toward the ajna chakra between the eyebrows. This pose relieves tension in the neck and face, stimulates the thyroid, and helps to rid the body of toxins.

## ꙩ The Story of Narasimha

The lion is widely regarded as the king of animals. Apart from men and their fabricated weapons, this fearless and powerful animal has no natural enemies. In the yoga tradition, the lion is best known as one of the avatars of Vishnu. He is named Narasimha, which means half man (*nara*), half lion (*simha*). The story of Narasimha as narrated in the Bhagavata Purana offers valuable spiritual insights.

In ancient times there lived a demonic ruler by the name of Hiranyakashipu. He gained great powers because of the tremendous penances he had performed. After Hiranyakashipu stood on his toes for one hundred years, Brahma had no other choice but to grant him a wish. Hiranyakashipu asked for immortality, but Brahma could not grant him this wish, since he himself was mortal. So Hiranyakashipu tried asking for immortality indirectly. He asked Brahma to give his assurance that he would not be killed during the day or night, inside or outside, in the sky or on the ground. He also asked that he not be killed by any weapon or any living being created by Brahma. After his desire was granted, Hiranyakashipu became ruler of the three worlds, consisting of the heavenly, middle, and hellish realms.

Hiranyakashipu became extremely violent against all the demigods and sages, who suffered greatly as a result. As a last resort, the demigods went to see Vishnu to ask for his protection. Vishnu promised that he would kill Hiranyakashipu if he ever turned his anger on his own saintly son, Prahlad. The sage-like youngster Prahlad had learned about the science of yoga while he was still in his mother's womb as she was being instructed by her teacher.

Hiranyakashipu sent his son Prahlad to the best available demon teachers to be instructed on the subjects of politics and general crookedness. Prahlad did not like the teachings. In the breaks between the lessons, he explained the science of yoga to his fellow demon schoolboys, who lost all their interest in politics and had a change of heart, much to the distress of their demon teachers.

When five-year-old Prahlad came to court one day, his father asked him in front of the royal assembly of miscreants to recount the best thing he had learned so far. Prahlad answered, "Oh king of the demons, I think it is best to renounce home and kingdom, which is like a prison, and go to the forest to practice yoga and meditate on Vishnu."

When Hiranyakashipu heard this answer and the name of his enemy Vishnu, he became mad with rage. He ordered his followers to kill Prahlad at once. They hesitated because Prahlad was merely a child, and in ancient times, even demons had some morals. But they were afraid of Hiranyakashipu and tried to execute his order. First they fed Prahlad poison, but it did not affect the boy. Then they threw him off a mountain, but that did not hurt him either. They buried him in a ditch, attacked him with spears, threw him in a fire, and tried to starve him—all in vain. Prahlad had the mystical protection of Vishnu, and no one was able to kill him. Finally they brought him back to his father.

Prahlad was standing before Hiranyakashipu with his hands in namaste mudra, showing respect to his father despite his demonic behavior. Hiranyakashipu fumed, "You dull-headed boy! Everybody is afraid of me. Why aren't you? I shall send you to your death right now! Who has given you this strength?"

Prahlad replied, "All strength comes from God. The only foe we have is our uncontrolled mind, which is afflicted by the six enemies of lust (*kama*), anger (*krodha*), greed (*lobha*), delusion (*moha*), envy (*mada*), and laziness (*matsarya*). They create dualities and make us divide the world into friends and foes. Those who have conquered their mind see nothing as their enemy. Only the ignorant believe others to be their enemy."

Hiranyakashipu became more enraged and shouted, "You foolish boy! You certainly want to die. There is no other God but me. And if there is, tell me, where is he?"

"Father, he is everywhere," Prahlad replied.

"Then why do I not see him in this pillar?" Hiranyakashipu countered.

"I see him in this pillar, Father," Prahlad replied.

"Oh really? Then let your pillar take this!" Hiranyakashipu shouted and gave a powerful blow to the pillar with his sword.

Then a terrible roaring sound emerged from the pillar, which shook the earth and the heavens and scared even Hiranyakashipu.

A minute later, Narasimha burst from the pillar. He fought for a while with Hiranyakashipu, the way a cat plays with a mouse, and then killed him by ripping open his guts with his sharp claws. So as to honor Brahma's promise to Hiranyakashipu, Narasimha did this neither in daytime nor at night, but at dusk; neither inside nor outside the house, but on the threshold; and neither in the sky nor on the ground, but on his lap.

After he killed the demon, no one was able to calm the fury of Narasimha, not even Shiva. Then all the demigods asked Prahlad to appease Narasimha, which the boy did successfully by reciting beautiful prayers.

By killing Hiranyakashipu, Narasimha had killed the six enemies of the mind that stand in the way of liberation. Narasimha is recognized as one who takes away the obstacles on the path of devotion.

## ∽ Slaying the Demons of Our Mind

The inspirational Prahlad was not disturbed by his father's demonic behavior. He calmly spoke the truth with a well-balanced mind. Prahlad understood that there are no demons in any kind of definitive way. There is only demonic behavior, which we may condemn, but we should not condemn the doer. Harmful behavior is born out of ignorance. Even Hiranyakashipu had the light of divinity within himself, although he chose to ignore it. Through their association with Prahlad, the demon boys actually changed in character.

When we perform simhasana, we may be reminded of the fearlessness we need on the path of yoga and also the fearlessness that develops from our practice. And we embody Narasimha by slaying the demons of our mind.

# poses of the sages

THE YOGIC TRADITION has always been filled with the wisdom and teachings of sages. Old texts give accounts of many sages who meditated on the banks of the sacred Ganges River, trying to find answers to the secret of life, the soul, and the universe. Who are we? Where have we come from? What is our destiny?

The sages' questions were prompted by their realization that life in the material world is ultimately temporary and filled with affliction. Disease, old age, and death are always hovering in the background, ready to poison man's cup of joy. Throughout history men and women have tried to free themselves from the limitations and suffering that accompany life in the mundane realm. The search for abiding peace and happiness and the quest for the reunion of the soul with the Divine gave birth to the great schools of yoga.

In Sanskrit the word for sage is *sadhu*. It refers to one who pursues and understands ultimate truth (*sat*). Sages have compiled yogic literature, which mostly narrates the lives and teachings of other sages. The stereotype of a sadhu is an old, half-naked man with matted hair who roams the Himalayas. In actuality a sage comes in many guises. He or she may be a child, a beggar, or a king. Regardless of his or her physical appearance, attributes include forbearance; an egalitarian vision; loving kindness; freedom from hatred, greed, and delusion; and a detachment from material objects.

"Sadhu" can also be traced to the Sanskrit root *sādh*, which means "to reach one's goal." This same root also appears in the word *sadhana*, which means "conscious spiritual practice." A sadhu is someone who has gained perfection in sadhana. Sadhana is indispensable for reaching the main goal of yoga, which can be described as enlightenment or self-realization.

While we don't necessarily know why each specific pose is attributed to a particular sage, we do know that sages have often put forth a huge amount of sadhana in order to reach enlightenment and benefit future yoga practitioners. Most sage-related postures are very difficult, and this may be to reflect the rigorous practice and sacrifices that the sages endured, efforts which continue to benefit yoga practitioners today.

# bharadvajasana

## HALF-LOTUS SEATED TWIST

*Bharadvajasana* is a challenging twist that is full of grace when fully accomplished. One leg is in half *virasana* (leg bent with the foot on the outside of the hip, toes pointing backward), and the other leg is in a half lotus position (foot high up on the inner thigh, with the knee moving toward the floor). The practitioner takes a deep twist toward the leg that is in half lotus, and the hand on the same side reaches back to grab the big toe, completing the twist.

The intensity of this particular posture is reflective of the story of the sage Bharadvaja.

## ✂ Too Much Study

Bharadvaja was a dedicated student. In fact, no one was more dedicated than he to the study of the Vedas. The most ancient of spiritual and philosophical texts, the Vedas encompass a vast body of knowledge. No one had ever expected to master them all—except the ambitious Bharadvaja. He devoted his whole life to the study of these texts: reading them, writing them down, committing them to memory, and then doing it all over again. So intense was his dedication that he exhausted one entire lifetime to the study of the Vedas.

Upon his rebirth, Bharadvaja knew immediately which path in life he wanted to follow—again, the study of the Vedas. As soon as he was able, he began his study of the sacred texts, believing that his intense focus and study would bring him closer to a higher power. Once again he studied so much that he exhausted another lifetime.

The third rebirth brought more of the same. People began to hear of this incredibly reclusive but extraordinarily wise sage named Bharadvaja. No one had ever seen him, because he spent his days and nights doing nothing but studying the Vedas. He was, by far, the most accomplished expert on the Vedas because he was the only one who had spent three whole lifetimes in such constant dedication to the scriptures!

At the end of his third lifetime, as Bharadvaja lay sick and dying in his bed, reciting Vedic mantras over and over and waiting for the end, Shiva appeared to him. Bharadvaja's eyes widened in surprise. He thought he had finally been liberated from the cycle of death and rebirth because of all his dedicated study. Unfortunately, he was in for another shock.

"Bharadvaja," said Shiva, with a disappointed tone in his voice. "What are you doing?"

"I'm dying, Shiva. Aren't you here to take me with you?" replied Baradhvaja with so much hope that his eyes sparkled.

"No, Bharadvaja, I won't be taking you with me this time, and I hope that you'll finally learn your lesson about all this outrageous studying you've been doing!" said Shiva, exasperated.

"What are you talking about? I've done so much studying only in the hopes of getting closer to you, Dear," replied the astonished Bharadvaja.

"Well," Shiva explained, "what you have learned is no more than this."

Shiva casually reached out the window and scooped up a handful of dirt from a nearby mountain and showed it to

Bharadvaja. "This is what you learned during the first lifetime of study." He placed the mound of dirt at Bharadvaja's bedside.

Then he reached out again and grabbed a second handful of dirt from another nearby mountain and showed it to Bharadvaja. "This is what you learned during the second lifetime of study." He placed the second mound next to the first.

Finally, he reached out and grabbed another handful of dirt from the closest mountain and showed it to the now bleary-eyed Bharadvaja. "This is what you learned during the third lifetime of study." He placed the final mound of dirt next to the others.

Shiva looked compassionately at Bharadvaja, placed his hand on his shoulder, and said, "You've spent all this time becoming the expert on the Vedas, and there is no doubt that no one knows more about them than you. But what you have actually learned is only a handful compared to the mountain of information that is still left to be learned, and what has all this study gotten you? Here you are, living alone, you have nothing joyful to show for your life, and you've shared your knowledge with no one. While you may know the Vedas, you don't understand their true meaning, because you have never bothered to share their grace and joy with others. It is through sharing this wisdom that it will truly come alive and live inside you.

"So, dear Bharadvaja, I'm going to give you another chance. You can spend one more lifetime trying to get close to my presence, and if you use it wisely, I promise you that it will be your last." And with that, Shiva left Bharadvaja, who died quietly that night.

Bharadvaja's next lifetime was spent not studying, but teaching. He dedicated himself to sharing the deep wisdom and joy that comes from the Vedas, and he educated many aspirants in the ways of the spiritual path. His knowledge and compassion was known far and wide, and people from different classes were proud to call him their teacher. When he was on his deathbed, students came from many distant lands to pay homage to the great Bharadvaja.

Even Shiva came to pay his respects to this venerable teacher. Once again, Shiva put his hand on Bharadvaja's shoulder and said,

"Dear Bharadvaja, you have finally learned your lesson. Do you see now how the wisdom of the Vedas is not contained within the knowing, but in the living and sharing of the wisdom? Look how many souls are alight because of your grace and generosity. You have done what I suggested, and now, as promised, if you wish, you may be liberated from the cycle of birth and rebirth."

Bharadvaja looked up at Shiva with joyful tears in his eyes and replied, "Shiva, while there is no one who resides more fully within my heart than yourself, I must respectfully decline your offer. You see, I now know that I can never be more close to you than when I share moments of joy with others by connecting with them through these sacred texts. Living this great wisdom is more of a heaven than I could ever ask for."

And so, with pride shining in his eyes, Shiva left Bharadvaja's bedside. And with joy in his heart, Bharadvaja left his body, only to be reborn as one of the greatest sages ever known.

## ꙮ A Sage's Wisdom

It took Bharadvaja three lifetimes to realize what, hopefully, we will learn in less than one: When we find the source of our joy, it is our duty to live it and share it with others. This doesn't mean we need to try to convince others to be joyful. Rather, if we live the lessons we have been taught, our example can inspire others to find that source of joy within themselves. Many people spend a lot of time doing something that makes them unhappy, or focusing so hard on achieving a goal that they miss the whole point.

Although it wasn't until Bharadvaja's fourth lifetime that he figured out how to actually live his life fully, maybe we can take the wisdom of this sage to heart in this intense twisting pose and begin to live our lives in a way that reflects the most important lesson of his story: When we find our true life's passion, it will be fully expressed when we begin to share it with others.

# koundinyasana

## STRAIGHT LEGS SIDE CROW POSE

This challenging arm balance requires both strength and flexibility; one leg reaches forward over the corresponding arm and the other leg extends back. Many students struggle for some time with the particulars of this posture before finding the proper balance required to lift themselves above the earth.

*Koundinyasana* has a variation, *parivritta* ("revolved") *koundinyasana*. This posture is easily reached from a *parivritta bakasana*, or side crane pose. Both legs are extended at opposite angles while the body is in a twisted position. Meeting the challenges of both versions of this posture requires a belief in oneself, which is the main lesson of the story about the great sage Koundinya.

## ◟◞ Prediction & Predicament

When King Suddhodana and Queen Maya welcomed Siddhartha, their first baby boy, into the world, they held a splendid gathering to bless the new prince. The most venerable sages and seers of the day arrived at court and, as was the custom, made predictions about the great things the little prince would accomplish in his lifetime. One by one, the wise men stepped up to tell the king and queen about the future of their son.

One sage said, "He will grow to become the greatest king that has ever ruled the land and will restore peace once and for all!"

Another holy man said, "The prince will bring wealth and prosperity, the likes of which has never been seen before in this kingdom!"

Another seer said, "This prince will be married to the most beautiful woman the world has ever known, and they will have so many sons that this royal lineage will live on for the rest of time!"

The king was pleased to hear all of these wonderful predictions, because he also believed that his son would surpass his own successful reign. But there was one more seer left to make a prediction. The wise Koundinya had served the court for a very long time, and the king and queen trusted him with many matters of state, so they were excited to hear what he might have to say.

Koundinya stood up and said, "My dear king and queen, I am pleased to inform you that your son will become one of the greatest kings to ever live, and he will preside over a kingdom far bigger than you can ever know, and for far longer than you or I could ever imagine. However, he will not do this by sitting upon a throne. In fact, your son, the Prince Siddhartha, will renounce the throne you call a throne, and he will leave this kingdom you call a kingdom, and he will walk away from his family. In doing so, he will discover

the path to happiness and truth. This discovery will lead him to become one of the most beloved figures the world will ever come to know."

The thought of his son renouncing everything the king had worked for both frightened and infuriated the king. He immediately threw Koundinya out of the court and banished him from the kingdom. On his way out the door, Koundinya said calmly, "On the day your son becomes enlightened, I will be there. And I will be the first to call him Buddha, the enlightened one." King Suddhodana decided right then and there that he would never let Koundinya's predictions come true.

As the baby prince grew into Siddhartha the man, King Suddhodana and Queen Maya protected and sheltered their son from the outside world. They never let him leave the palace. They made sure to employ only young and healthy people, so that Siddhartha would never be exposed to suffering, sickness, or death. When Siddhartha became a young man, he pressured his father into letting him leave the palace. Despite his father's nervousness, a day was arranged for Siddhartha to see the world for the first time.

The king had ordered everyone who was sick or old to be hidden from sight. He also ordered that all traces of death be removed from his son's parade route, and that the city be cleared of ascetics, so as not to give his son any aspiration toward the ascetic wanderings predicted by Koundinya. As Siddhartha made his way through the streets of the city, he saw only young and beautiful people, and he thought the world was only filled with good health, joy, and ease. This is all he had ever known. But as he rounded a corner, he looked down an alley and saw a hint of something different.

Prince Siddhartha broke off the parade route and snuck down the alley, where he found the people on the lowest rungs of society trying to hide from view. This was the first time in his life that the prince encountered death, old age, and sickness. He also found an ascetic, who was trying desperately to escape this suffering that Siddhartha had only just realized was a part of life.

As soon as Siddhartha returned to the palace, he knew what his mission in life must be. And so he snuck off in the middle of the night to begin a life of wandering and trying to find a way to end the suffering of humanity. At the edge of his kingdom, Koundinya was waiting for him.

For many years, Koundinya and Prince Siddhartha practiced severe asceticism to liberate themselves from attachments to body and mind and, as a result, reach the end of suffering. Despite all their self-denial, Siddhartha only found that he was suffering more. One day, he decided asceticism wasn't the way to find enlightenment, which greatly frustrated Koundinya, who believed it was the only way. So the sage and the prince parted ways.

This was when Prince Siddhartha began to discover the Middle Way, or the path of Buddhism. Upon his enlightenment, he sought out Koundinya to tell him about the four noble truths. Koundinya realized immediately that Siddhartha had become the Buddha—the enlightened one. He knew that Siddhartha's Middle Path had led him to nirvana, and this time, Koundinya became Siddhartha's student. Koundinya and the Buddha began to spread the teachings of enlightenment, showing others that the greatest kingdom one can have dominion over is the realm of the heart.

## Divine Realization

The Buddha's story is one of inevitability, providence, and perseverance. His realization of "Buddha-hood" was the result of his intense desire to alleviate the suffering of the world. What he discovered in his enlightened state were the founding principles of Buddhism, known as the four noble truths. They are as follows:

- To live is to suffer.
- Desire is the root of suffering.
- It is possible to stop suffering.
- The way to stop suffering is by following the Middle Path, which incorporates eight principles: right understanding, right thought, right speech, right action, right livelihood, right effort, right mindfulness, and right concentration.

The Buddha discovered the Middle Way, but even his staunchest supporter, Koundinya, didn't immediately recognize the truth of his teachings. A little skepticism can go a long way on the spiritual path, and questioning one's teachers can give one confidence in the path one finally chooses. Koundinya's pose reflects this difficult pathway to grace. It's considered a challenging pose, but it is simply a question of balance—the middle way between effort and grace.

# vasisthasana

## PLANK POSE

Sometimes called side plank pose, *Vasisthasana*
is a challenging arm balance that strengthens all
the major muscle groups of the body—arms, legs,
core, and spine. The practitioner balances on one
arm, with the body straight and the feet flexed
sideways on the floor.

## ～ Even Kings Need Inspiration

Vasistha was a great sage who took up the challenge of being a teacher to King Ram, who is one of the avatars of Vishnu. Ram appeared on earth to restore the path of righteousness, or *dharma*, which had become corrupted by negative influences.

Ram's father, King Dasharatha, was concerned for his young son after he returned from some travels and seemed really disillusioned with the state of the world. Ram's apathy was uncharacteristic, and King Dasharatha hoped the revered sage Vasistha would be able to help. When Dasharatha described Ram's state of mind to Vasistha, the wise sage was actually pleased to hear about it, because he knew that the kind of dispassion young Ram was experiencing was actually a precursor to the spiritual path. One must first see cracks in the ceiling before one can start to see the light shining through it. Vasistha saw Ram's discomfort as an opportunity and went to Ram to introduce himself.

Ram expressed skepticism at the great sage's ability to lift his spirits. He was in a deep depression, and it seemed as if the whole world had lost its luster. Vasistha began explaining that this dulled vision was precisely what was needed to regain his clarity, and that he had already begun on his spiritual path. He just needed some guidance and direction, which a good teacher could provide.

As many of us know, sometimes we have to hit rock bottom before we can begin our journey back out into the light. It is this soul who is interested in transformation and sees where things could be better in the world that is best suited for spiritual pursuits. This doesn't mean that we aren't content with the way things are, but that we are not content with that which doesn't serve our spiritual practice. When we realize this subtle difference, as Vasistha explained to Ram, we can use the processes of yoga to be more and more content while letting go of what no longer serves us.

## ◯ Lesson of Liberation

The dialogue between Ram as a student and Vasistha as a teacher comprises the Yoga Vasistha, one of the foremost texts in yoga philosophy and mythology. It is in this text that we learn about the state of the jivanmukta, the soul who is liberated while living. The jiva is the individual soul, the unique person who expresses himself or herself through work, family, career, talent, and passions. *Mukti* is a Sanskrit word for "liberation" or "freedom." It refers to freedom from the mind's continual insistence that one is merely mortal and its difficulty in recognizing the divinity that lies within us. The magic occurs, explained Vasistha, when the individual soul merges with absolute freedom, so we can be, as the saying goes, in this world, but not of this world.

## ◯ Crows & Coconuts

One recurring metaphor within the Yoga Vasistha is that of the crow and the coconut. Vasistha encourages Ram in the same way the Buddha encourages us to "act as if everything you do makes a world of difference, knowing all the while that everything you do makes no difference to the world." Yoga is full of these kinds of paradoxes. In this case, Vasistha talks about the crow who alights on a tree, and at the same moment, a coconut falls to the ground. Now, does the crow's momentum cause the coconut to fall? Or, is it just the coconut's time to fall, which coincides with the exact moment the crow lands on the tree? Vasistha poses this question to Ram several times. It refers to an idea found throughout many yogic scriptures, such as the Bhagavad Gita: We are entitled to the action, but not to the fruits of that action.

We can think of the world as a great practice ground or perhaps a proctored exam, in which the universe is giving us the opportunity to get it right. Whether it is our actions that cause coconuts to fall or it is simply the coconut's time doesn't really matter. What matters is that we continue to apply our actions—our thoughts, words, and deeds—so that we can hopefully influence

more coconuts. We never know when the random comment of kindness will touch a friend's heart. It may be their time to receive that kindness, or it may be our utterance of it, but either way, it's important to our spiritual progress that we speak. It's important that we never give up hope that our uplifted actions will change the world, even if it is just the world's time to change.

## ∿ Vasistha's Legacy

After his great lesson from Vasistha, Ram went on to be one of the most renowned kings in history, as well as the main character in the great epic the Ramayana. His pursuit of equality and happiness for all his people; his great love of his partner, Sita; and the bravery of his best friend, Hanuman, who rescues Sita from a demon, are all well-loved tales. None of these would have been possible without the patience and teachings of Vasistha. He was persistent in offering his wisdom to young Ram, and Ram was open and willing to receive his teaching.

So the crow and the coconut work together to make fate happen. For yogis, there is no such thing as luck. There is only being in the right place at the right time, after doing a lot of preparation so that all the elements fall perfectly into place.

# astavakrasana

## EIGHT ANGLE POSE

*Astavakrasana* is named after the sage Astavakra, whose body was bent (*vakra*) in eight (*asta*) places. The pose reflects the crooked profile of the sage. Astavakrasana is an arm balance that involves extending one leg over the corresponding arm, extending the other below it, and crossing the ankles. When the body leans forward, and the elbows are bent, the act of squeezing and straightening the legs allows the seat to lift off the floor. This challenging pose strengthens arms, wrists, and abdominal muscles.

## ~ᴐ The Story of Astavakra

While in his mother's womb, Astavakra used to hear his father reciting the mantras of the Vedas. Astavakra's father sometimes mispronounced words, which made Astavakra wince and twist in pain. When he could not take it anymore, he corrected his father by speaking from the belly of his mother. His father took offense and cursed Astavakra, which caused his body to bend in eight places. And so he was born with a crippled body.

One day when he was grown, Astavakra decided to go the court of King Janaka to hear the philosophical discussions that went on in the assembly. King Janaka was the father of Ram's lovely Sita. Famed for his knowledge of the Vedas, the king invited learned scholars to his court. Because Astavakra's body was so deformed, it took him many days to make the journey to King Janaka's court with the help of a walking stick.

When Astavakra entered the court, the whole assembly started to laugh at the sight of his crooked body. But to everyone's surprise, Astavakra broke into what they thought was intense laughter. He seemed to be laughing harder and louder than anyone else.

King Janaka approached Astavakra and asked, "Who are you, and why is it you are laughing so loudly?"

Astavakra answered, "Actually, I am not laughing, but rather crying. I have come from so far away despite my bad physical condition. I heard that in your court were men of great wisdom. I have come with high hopes to hear their enlightened discussions. But I have been very disappointed. I was hoping to find great yogis here, but I have made my journey in vain because I have only found shoemakers in your assembly."

King Janaka replied, "Why do you think that everyone here is a shoemaker? Don't you think anyone here is learned, or has

come from a great dynasty of Brahmans, or has great knowledge of the Vedas?"

"No," Astavakra said. "They are all shoemakers. They see only skin. They do not see the *atma*, the soul. They have no realization of the soul and the Supreme Soul. They merely see the surface, and base their judgments solely on this. This is the occupation of a cobbler, who is always saying: 'This skin is good; that skin is not good. This one is smooth; that one is rough.' Coming here has been a waste of time."

King Janaka and his assembly became deeply embarrassed at Astavakra's words, realizing the truth of his sentiments. King Janaka bowed down to Astavakra and became his student. Astavakra then gave him lessons in the science of the soul, which were recorded as the Astavakra Gita.

## ∽ Astavakra's Wisdom

This story points to an all-too-common human condition. Most of us are overly concerned with external appearance, and sometimes we even derive our whole identity from it. Although yoga regards the body as the temple of the soul, which needs to be taken care of properly, it also reminds us that we are much more than just our physical appearance. It is therefore not a bad idea to cultivate a healthy amount of detachment from it. How much do we identify with our body? Does our world end when we discover a pimple or a grey hair in the mirror? The story of Astavakra shows that external appearance does not say very much about what lives in the heart, and we may easily be misguided.

The story of Astavakra also demonstrates that we can practice yoga no matter what the state of our body. Our flexibility is measured not by the length of our muscles, but by our willingness to step up to our challenges. The great sage Astavakra exemplified this attitude by not letting his crippled body get in the way of his pursuit of yoga. The pose astavakrasana does not necessarily require a lot of flexibility or strength, but it does require the kind of lift that comes from pulling oneself up by the heart strings. The most important muscles to flex are those of the heart.

# vishvamitrasana

## SIDE ANGLE BALANCE

Twist, standing pose, hip opener, and arm balance all in one, *vishvamitrasana* seems as challenging as the life of the sage Vishvamitra. Beginning in downward-facing dog pose, vishvamitrasana is performed by bringing the right leg forward around the outside of the right arm. The arm is then tucked completely under the thigh. With an exhale one leans on to the right hand to balance with the left arm on the left thigh. On the inhale the left arm is raised and the right leg is extended.

## ◯ The Life of Vishvamitra

Vishvamitra was a king before he became a great sage. Legend has it that on one of his military journeys, King Vishvamitra reached the hermitage of the great sage Vasistha. The sage took care of Vishvamitra's entire army, feeding them to their heart's content. When King Vishvamitra asked the sage Vasistha how he could feed so many people, the sage replied that his magical cow was responsible. Amazed by the ability of this fantastic animal, Vishvamitra asked for the cow as a gift. Vasistha refused, and so Vishvamitra decided to challenge Vasistha to a battle over the amazing cow.

Despite King Vishvamitra's great strength, he was easily defeated by the sage Vasistha's mystical powers. The king realized that the sage's strength was actually far greater than that of a mere warrior. So, he decided to give up his kingdom and try to become a sage himself through the practice of yoga.

The practicing yogi Vishvamitra was known for his bad temper. He often cursed people, diminishing the yogic powers he had obtained through so much hard work and practice. One day, while Vishvamitra was meditating to gain spiritual power, Indra, the king of the demigods, became fearful that Vishvamitra might overthrow him. He sent an incredibly beautiful woman to Vishvamitra, who became so enchanted that they began an affair.

Eventually, Vishvamitra realized that his lustful pursuits had thrown him off track, and he resumed his meditation. After a lot of concentration and intense practice, the yogi Vishvamitra finally became the sage Vishvamitra. He ultimately embodied all the qualities of a sage, such as patience, forgiveness, and compassion, and even his former enemy, Vasistha, came to greatly respect him.

## Trial & Error

Vishvamitra's journey shows that progress in life often involves trial and error, and that persistence will lead to success. This is also what Krishna assures Arjuna in the Bhagavad Gita, when Arjuna tells Krishna that controlling his mind seems more difficult than controlling the wind. At first our temper may prevent us from progressing on our spiritual path. But if we fall on the ground, we can stand up with its help. Because Vishvamitra's *sadhana* (spiritual practice) was fraught with more difficulty than Vasistha's, his pose is more difficult, too—a reminder that yoga isn't always an easy path, but certainly one worth pursuing.

# animals & earth

| | | | |
|---|---|---|---|
| Matsyasana |  | Hamsasana |  |
| Matsyendrasana |  | Tadasana |  |
| Chandrasana |  | Vrikshasana |  |
| Ardha Chandrasana |  | Gomukhasana |  |
| Bhujangasana |  | Bakasana |  |
| Mayurasana |  | Shavasana |  |

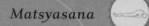

THE YOGA TRADITION is one that brings the practitioner close to nature. One of our main duties as yogis is to remove obstacles that separate us from the divine spark that lies within all things. The most accessible forms to practice this principle with are the beings and things that exist all around us. We look for the similarities in the tree, the dog, the cat, and the cow, and by assuming those postures, we create relationships with the different embodied forms of life on earth.

As the story of the fish pose tells us, the very first yogi was Shiva. He is said to be the originator of the yoga tradition, and we honor him in many ways through our practice. One of the original forms of Shiva is Pashupati, the protector of the animals. Sharon Gannon and David Life, cofounders of Jivamukti Yoga, say that the yogi is the "original tree hugger," the one who finds inherent value in remaining connected to the Earth, the plants, the animals, and all the beings and things that surround us on this planet. As Pashupati, Shiva walked softly among the beings of the earth, and they all saw him as a friend.

There is something powerful about allowing one's heart to be so open that other beings can sense it. For the most part, human beings find it difficult to recognize this openness in others, but animals can sense it right away. They know instinctively whether someone is there to help or harm them.

Many yoga postures give us the opportunity to release fear from our hearts, including balance postures, which challenge our fear of falling; inversions, which challenge our fear of turning the world upside down; and backbends, which challenge our fear of fully opening to the moment. When fear exerts its grip, it can be an overpowering force that keeps us closed and therefore separated from the brilliant opportunities to connect that constantly surround us.

The lesson of how to become fearless always lies within the pose itself. Whether it's through a rich story like that of Hanuman and his brave nature, or the simplicity of the dog that trusts its owner, or the crane that flies free and wild, we have much to learn from our fellow earthlings. Many of them exist without constant fear, going about their daily lives and instinctive habits without thinking, "Gosh, I wish I had done that differently."

There's a striking contrast between the way humans hold on to fear and the way animals freely let go of it. In the wild, when a tiger tries to feast on a gazelle, but just misses his catch, the spared gazelle doesn't dwell on his near-fatal experience for weeks. He doesn't run to all of his gazelle friends and recount the story, and he doesn't stop going to the watering hole for fear of another attack. He simply shakes his whole body, literally moving the experience through his physical form, and goes about his life.

Asanas give us the opportunity to do just the same. We get the chance to move our life experience through our body by taking the shapes of the various forms in nature. We stretch and create space in our joints and muscles and do our best to embody the essence of each posture, learning its inherent lessons and experiencing freedom in that form. When this process takes hold and begins to release the fear from our body and our heart, we are able to live our lives joyfully, moment by moment. Fear lives in us as tension, and asana postures are designed to release tension from our bodies. The absence of tension is the absence of fear. And the absence of fear signifies the presence of joy, love, and open-heartedness. As we embody these shapes of nature, we learn to fall in love with the world around us.

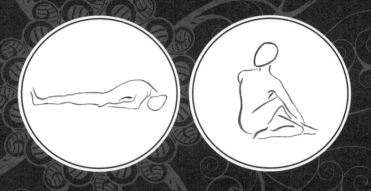

# matsyasana & matsyendrasana

## FISH POSE

In *matsyasana,* or fish pose, the practitioner lies on the back, with legs extended and engaged and elbows drawn beneath the body. An inhale lifts the chest toward the ceiling, while the head drops back and the crown touches the floor. Just as there are many types of fish in the sea, there are many variations of this pose. In one variation the legs are in a lotus position, or a bound angle (*baddha konasana*) position. In another, the legs are lifted off the ground at a 45-degree angle to the floor, and the arms are lifted so they are parallel to the legs, with the palms pressing together. Alternatively, the supported version of this posture can be done by placing a block lengthwise between the shoulder blades and allowing the head to rest on a blanket. *Matsyendrasana,* described in the following pages, honors the fish in an altogether different pose.

## The First Yoga Student

After ten thousand years of intense meditation, Shiva decided to descend from his seat upon Mount Kailash. As destroyer of the cosmos, Shiva rarely sees the need for personal upkeep, so he marched down the mountain, dreadlocked and encrusted with dirt, to find his beloved Parvati. As the consort of Shiva, Parvati has a lot of time for the particulars, and she had a feeling that this would be the day of Shiva's return. So she packed a picnic and went to meet him at the river. As she was setting out lunch, her beloved arrived.

Shiva announced to Parvati that while he was upon his meditation seat, he discovered the most wondrous thing. After so many years of meditation, he was granted the key to the universe, the secret to salvation. He had discovered yoga, the path to ultimate union between the individual self and the divine source. As he went on an on about the amazing teachings he had conjured up on the mountaintop, Parvati continued fretting about lunch.

"Parvati, aren't you listening to me?" exclaimed Shiva.

"What? Oh, sorry, my love. I'm just getting lunch ready." Parvati coolly responded.

"But I've just made the discovery of a lifetime. Are you not interested in hearing about it?" Shiva asked, puzzled over her apparently flippant attitude about his great discovery.

"Of course I am. Please go on," she simply replied.

So Shiva continued with his discourse on yoga: how it works, what kind of practices one can do to rediscover it, what a state of meditation is like, and how the individual contains a piece of the divine source. Little did Shiva know that Parvati had known about yoga for time immemorial and had been practicing in her own quiet, devout way for as long as she could remember. Somehow she

had always assumed that Shiva knew about yoga, too, but had failed to mention it. While she was a bit surprised to learn that Shiva had only just "discovered" yoga, she was humble enough to let him have his moment and kept listening as Shiva rambled on about the glories of the practice.

Meanwhile, in the nearby river a fish was swimming downstream. *Matsya* (matsya is Sanskrit for "fish") was a special fish who had a knack for listening carefully. As he swam by Shiva and Parvati he overheard some of Shiva's remarks and decided to stay a little while and listen. He had never heard Shiva lecture on the nature of life and the universe before, and his words sounded important.

Shiva spoke, and Matsya listened. And as he listened, something magical began to happen. He felt the techniques and theory of yoga begin to take hold of his body and live inside of him. Through his perfect listening to Shiva's instructions, Matsya became enlightened by the conclusion of Shiva's discourse. At that moment, Shiva became the first *guru* ("teacher") and Matsya became the first *chela* ("student"). They began the long lineage of teachers and students who successfully passed the teachings of yoga down through an oral tradition over thousands of years. Nothing in yoga is more important than this relationship, and through perfect listening, any good student can follow in the footsteps of Matsya.

## ⌒◡ The Return of the Fish

When someone becomes truly enlightened, he or she has an opportunity to return to earth in order to help the rest of us who are interested in this kind of liberation. Matsya chose to come back, and he was born, as legend tells it, as half fish, half human. He was called Matsyendranath, "the lord of the fishes." It is his wisdom that resulted in the the Hatha Yoga Pradipika, written by the Nath yogis. As as result, all hatha yogis can trace their lineage all the way back to Matsyendranath's teachings.

We honor the fish and his return as Matsyendranath, in the seated spinal twist, matsyendrasana. In this posture, the upright torso resembles that of the half human sage, whereas the folded legs represent a fish's tail. This pose is one that keeps us connected to the strong lineage of teachers that have either directly or indirectly influenced us, because as this story shows, we all come from the same roots.

# chandrasana &
# ardha chandrasana

## MOON & HALF MOON POSE

*Chandrasana*, or moon pose, is done in a standing lunge position, with the back knee off the floor. The arms reach up, and the spine stays long. *Ardha chandrasana*, or half-moon pose, is also a standing posture, but it requires more balance and attention. While standing on one foot with the corresponding hand on the floor, the practitioner stretches out the body, reaches back with the other leg, and reaches up with the free hand. Eventually, he or she turns the head to look at the sky.

## Ganesh & the Moon

Ganesh, the charming elephant-headed god adored by so many for his generous ways and clever antics, is also known for his wild infatuation with all things sweet. He is often depicted with a bowl of *prasad* (sweet, blessed food) in his palm, which he is never far from ingesting. Despite his love of sugary foods, he is a master of yoga, taking after his father, Shiva. Ganesh knows how to balance indulgences and austerities, leaving him with a flexible, albeit pudgy, figure.

On one of his exploits, Ganesh actually consumed so many sweet cakes that his belly was full to bursting. He decided it was time to head home and relax his stuffed belly, so he hopped on his trusty "steed," a tiny mouse. Because the mouse is such a small vehicle, Ganesh has to practice extraordinary balance to keep his hulking frame on the erratic creature.

The pair was cruising smoothly along when a very long cobra slithered onto their path and frightened the mouse. The mouse darted one way, and Ganesh fell the other. When he hit the ground, his overstuffed belly exploded and sweet cakes rained everywhere. This greatly perturbed Ganesh, who was upset not only by the cobra's disruption of his ride, but at the loss of the sweet fullness of his tummy. He walked around, collecting all the sweet cakes and stuffed them, one by one, back into his belly. Then he snatched up the cobra and tied it around his waist to cinch it shut. All the while, the moon, Chandra, was watching the extravaganza, and couldn't help exploding into laughter at Ganesh's crazy antics. Who, indeed, could resist?

Ganesh was very upset to be the object of Chandra's laughter, and in a fit of anger (remember, he is Shiva's son), he broke off his right tusk and hurled it at the moon. Pierced by the tusk, Chandra's

light went out. Ganesh cursed the moon so it would never shine again, leaving the earth continuously lit by the sun.

With no night, no dawn, and no dusk, love was lost to the world. There was no place for romance, and men and gods alike became scorched and hopeless upon the hot earth. Ganesh was holed up in his palace when a group of gods came to appeal to him to allow the moon to shine once more. Flattered by their appeals, Ganesh decided he could agree to a compromise. He would let the moon shine, but it would be required to wax and wane, shining at its full potential only once every four weeks. This, he decided, would be a permanent lesson for the moon so it would remember never to laugh at him again. As for Ganesh, he always carries the broken tusk that signifies his momentary rage at having lost his balance.

## The Moon's Lesson

One of the greatest lessons the yogi can learn is that everything we experience has an internal source of energy, as do the sun and moon (see chakrasana, page 30). Within our bodies, the sun and moon occupy opposing halves. The moon presides over the left energy channel (*ida nadi*), and the sun presides over the right one (*pingala nadi*). Ideally, we strive to seek a balance between both sources of light, basking in the moon as much as the sun and learning to wield both types of energy as we progress upon our path to enlightenment.

Ganesh may have taught Chandra a lesson, but the real lesson here is that steeped in only sunshine, all love is lost from the world. There is no softness, no shadow to define the landscape of our heart. Without a dawn or dusk, there is no halfway point in which to steal away during those wee hours of perfect balance between night and day. Within our yoga practice, we learn the truth of that age-old wisdom, "As above, so below. As without, so within,"—as with the sun and moon in the sky, so with those in our heart—and we seek to find as much joy in the shadow and lunar places of our existence as we do in the bright and solar places of our life.

# bhujangasana

## COBRA POSE

*Bhujangasana,* or cobra pose, is a simple backbend that resembles its namesake. As we lie on our belly and use the muscles of the back to lift our head and chest, our chest and upper arms represent the hood of the cobra. Because snakes have no limbs, the hands are traditionally not used to push oneself up higher.

## ↝ The Beauty of the Beast

The cobra is a fearsome creature for most, but it is the friend of the yogi. Its many manifestations can help us on the yogic path as we stumble over obstacles, poisons, and fear. Shiva, for one, adorns himself with cobras. He drapes them around his neck, signifying a deep familiarity with the fear of death, or *abhinivesha*.

The snake is a powerful symbol of our ability to relinquish all fears as we progress on a spiritual path. The way we give up fear is not by running from it, as some might do from the cobra, but by getting close to it and seeing it from a different perspective. Shiva's son, Ganesh, wears a cobra around his waist, not just as an homage to his father (or as a means to hold in his pudgy belly), but as a symbol of his attempt to follow in his father-teacher's footsteps. As a yoga disciple, Ganesh walks in his father's footsteps along the yogic path and shows his commitment to mastering his fears.

The cobra was also used by the gods to churn the ocean of nectar; they tugged on both ends to stir the pot. In the myth about the tortoise pose (page 90), the grip on the cobra by both the demigods and demons signified their mastery over their fear of death and their strong desire for immortality. It's similar to the Sanskrit chant:

> *Asato ma sadgamaya*
> *Tamaso ma jyotir gamaya*
> *Mrtyor ma amrtam gamaya*

This translates as "Lead me from the unreal to the real, from darkness into the light, from death to immortality." The cobra often symbolizes death because of its poisonous nature, but in grabbing hold of it, the demigods and demons found that it was actually their route to immortality.

## ∿ The Sound of the Snake

According to the Hatha Yoga Pradipika, the ultimate aim of the hatha yogi is to hear the internal sound, the most basic vibration, or as yogis call it, the *nadam*. According to scientists, every aspect of the universe is composed of tiny vibrating strings, which makes everything, from the cosmic to the subtle, vibrate.. Snakes have a built-in capacity to listen for subtle vibrations, and this amazing ability makes the cobra's potency as a yogic symbol even more powerful.

One often conjures an image of snake charmers at the thought of the cobra, and it has long been said that the music of the charmer calmed the vicious beast. What is true of snakes, however, is that they have no external ears. In order to hear sound, they must contact a hard surface with their jaw to conduct the vibration into their aural nerves. This means that the snake listens through internal means, rather than through external means as humans do. Snakes hear on a much more subtle level than the snake charmer's external sound, which is powerful, if one considers the potency of nadam, or internal sound.

## Lured by Spiritual Practice

While the great Buddha was meditating under the sacred *bodhi* tree, a group of cobras gathered nearby, lulled by his quiet calm and inner confidence. He sensed their presence but had no fear, and this fearlessness assured the snakes that he would remain still. His stillness was like a balm to their minds, and so they stayed close to him to protect him. Witnesses gathered around the Buddha but would not venture too close for fear of disturbing the den of deadly snakes surrounding him. When it began to rain, the people became distressed about the Buddha's soaking head, but they dared not go near to cover him. The snakes, in gratitude to him for providing a quiet space, devised a plan to protect the Buddha from the elements. The king of the cobras slithered up behind him and drew himself up as tall as he could, which was difficult given his limbless nature. When he was at his full height—a third of his body lifted completely off the earth—he opened his great hood and created a large canopy, under which the Buddha sat, sublimely peaceful, and continued his meditation. The observers gasped in awe at the generosity of the cobra, as well as the steadiness of the meditating Buddha.

# mayurasana

## PEACOCK POSE

*Mayurasana* represents the glorious peacock. This arm balance begins with the hands together on the floor, fingers pointing backward. Then, resting on the elbows, the practitioner leans forward in order to allow the legs to lift off the floor. The chest and head mimic the body of the peacock as the skyward-reaching legs represent its plumed tail.

## ⌒ The Fiercest Fighter

The star cluster Pleiades is personified by six heavenly sisters, who by Shiva's grace, each bore an identical son. When Shiva's consort, Parvati, learned of these six boys, she took them under her care and loved them with all her heart. With her intense adoration, she picked all six of them up and squeezed them so tightly that they morphed into one powerful baby with six heads. He was known by several names, including Kartikeya ("son of the Pleiades," which were called Kritika), and Shanmukh, which means "six-faced one."

When he was only a few months old, Kartikeya was already the fiercest fighter anyone had ever seen, and a very successful one. He chose the elegant peacock for his transportation because peacocks are also incredibly fierce fighters. They are the only enemy of cobras and are able to kill and eat the snakes, ingesting the powerful poison and transforming it into beauty and grace.

It so happened that before Kartikeya's birth, the king of the demons had completed a thousand years of penance to Brahma in order to ask him for a wish. When the demon asked Brahma to make him immortal, Brahma replied, "Nonsense! What is born always must die. This is an impossible wish. Ask of me something else."

This evil demon was very clever, and taking into account Shiva's long absences from his lover Parvati, he asked Brahma to only be killed by a seven-month-old son of Shiva, since it seemed unlikely they would ever have a son.

Brahma granted the demon's wish. Now that he was supposedly immortal, the evil demon felt powerful enough to throw all the gods out of heaven, taking it over for himself. He and his demon army demolished the place, and the gods became very upset.

It was right around Kartikeya's seventh month of age that the gods were suffering most from the evil demon's wrath. They noticed the cleverness and prowess of the swiftly growing child, and they pleaded with Shiva to let Kartikeya lead a war against the evil demon. Shiva obliged, knowing full well his son's strength and capabilities.

So, astride his lustrous steed, the peacock, Kartikeya led an army of gods and demigods into war to win the return of their rightful place in the heavens. The evil demon scoffed at the sight of young Kartikeya on his glorious bird and yelled across the battlefield, "Is the only one of you brave enough to challenge me a young boy? Send him home to play war games with his little toys and take your battle elsewhere!"

Just then, Kartikeya and the gods charged the field and attacked the demons. While the gods and demons fought, someone shouted to Kartikeya that he must be the one to kill the evil demon. He started for the demon with his peacock by his side and a great staff as his weapon. The battle ensued, testing both of them to their limits, but in the end, young Kartikeya prevailed and won the war that allowed the gods to go home to their heavenly abode.

## ‿ᴐ Feathers, Fearlessness & Faith

Kartikeya's peacock was a noble choice for a vehicle, or *vahana* in Sanskrit. As the god presiding over all wars, and one of exceptional knowledge, Kartikeya needed a steed that was his equal in strength and luminosity. We're all familiar with the peacock's regal qualities, but its ferocity comes as a surprise. As the only enemy of the king cobra, the peacock is able to strike fear into the heart of the venomous snake, when all other animals fear the snake for its deadly poison. As one who conquers the cobra, the peacock symbolizes conquering death, as Kartikeya does riding on his steed across the battlefield.

The peacock is more than a symbol of fearlessness. It also represents faithfulness as well as the quality of light. When a peacock's mate dies, it remains alone for the rest of its days, and legend has it that it often dies of a broken heart. But as it walks the earth proudly, yogis look to the peacock as a representation of the quality of lightness, or sattva guna. The peacock has neither the qualities of the *tamas* guna (heaviness and inertia) nor those of the *rajas* guna (vigor and impulsiveness). It leads its life with such regality and serenity that we often try to emulate those same beautiful qualities ourselves.

There is another pose attributed to the peacock, called *pincha mayurasana*, or peacock feather pose. It's more commonly known as a forearm balance. Pincha refers to a peacock feather. When the wind catches the feather, it lifts it straight up into the air, and we are to mimic that same lift and lightness in our own attempt at the asana. Again, lightness prevails here, and there is a double entendre because the pose asks us to be as light as air as we lift up and also as bright as the light of the peacock when we do our practice.

The peacock in yogic mythology is strongly linked with Krishna, who wears a peacock feather in his hair. The forest of Vrindavan, where he was born, abounds with peacocks. In the scriptures of devotional yoga, the dancing of the peacocks has been compared to the beautiful and masterful dancing of Krishna with the cowherd girls of Vrindavan, who represent the souls that are completely surrendered to Krishna as the personification of divine love. Likewise, the practice of asana, and in particular, mayurasana, expresses the yogi's desire to connect with the Divine in a dance of compassion.

## Digesting the Poison

The physical benefits of mayurasana are said to be the perfection (over time) of our digestive abilities, which mirrors the peacock's ability to digest the poison of the venomous cobra. The peacock can take the poison, assimilate it, and still be beautiful. We often have lots of poisons to ingest—not just in the form of actual food, but in situations and relationships as well. This pose helps us to process the poisons that might be contaminating our gut and also, through subtle shifts in perception, to transform the negativity of the world around us into beauty.

# hamsasana

## SWAN POSE

*Hamsasana*, or swan pose, is very similar to the peacock pose, except that the fingers face forward. The swan is considered to be a very regal bird. Mythology lauds it for its capacity to extract milk that has been mixed into water. Great yogis are sometimes referred to as *paramahamsa*, which literally means "topmost swans," because they are able to extract the spiritual essence from everything they encounter.

## ⌒ Vehicle of the Voice

Before the creation of the world, the great Brahma sat in meditation for long periods of time. Eventually his mind became filled with clarity, or what yogis would call *sattva* guna. While this quality of lightness was bubbling up in his mind, a girl was created and appeared before him.

Stunned by her magnificent beauty, Brahma asked her, "Who are you?"

She replied, "My name is Saraswati. Now that you've conjured me, I would love a proper seat and a divine purpose to fulfill."

Brahma gave her the most radiant lotus flower for a throne and the purest white swan and said that she would remain on the tip of the tongue of the most learned and artistic of beings to give them creative inspiration.

This is how the great goddess Saraswati came to be, with her knack for music, arts, and knowledge and her glorious swan for a vehicle. It is said that Saraswati presides over an ancient holy river in India of the same name, and that she controls the flow of its life-giving waters. Within her name and form, we also find the essence of *vak*, or speech, as Saraswati is the master of speech and communication.

The sacred *mantra* So'Ham is the mantra of the breath, what yogis call the *ajapa* mantra, or "the silent mantra." Every time we breathe, we are repeating this mantra. On the inhale we whisper "sssssssoooooooo," and on the exhale, "hhhhhaaaammmmmm." This occurs with more clarity when we apply ujayi, or "victorious breath," a type of breathing practice to focus the mind, so we can hear the sound as we make it. So'Ham is a contraction of the mantra *shiva aham*, which means "I am That," or literally, "Shiva, I am." By constantly repeating any mantra, we begin to take on its

inherent qualities, so as we pay attention to the ajapa mantra, we become more familiar with our divine nature.

The more we repeat So'Ham, the more difficult it is to hear where it begins and where it ends. Eventually So'Ham starts to sound like Ham'Sa, which is the Sanskrit name for the swan, the master of the breath. Because it is Saraswati's vehicle and she is the master of speech, we see how these two entities are linked and work together to make all of our utterances uplifted and sacred.

# tadasana

## MOUNTAIN POSE

*Tadasana* means "mountain pose." It is a basic standing pose with the feet together and the hands at the side of the body. This posture promotes the stillness, strength, relaxed power, and stability we associate with mountains.

## ꩜ The Himalaya

For a long time the Himalaya mountains have been populated by wandering sages and yogis, who considered the solitude of mountain caves to be ideal for the practice of yoga and meditation. Himalaya means abode (*alaya*) of snow (*hima*), but the highest mountain range on earth is also referred to as Devalaya, "the abode of the gods." According to yoga philosophy, within everything there is consciousness and quality—not only in humans and animals, but also in natural phenomena like rivers, mountains, and trees. The Himalaya are represented by the god Himavat, who is the father of Parvati, the consort of Shiva.

Mountains are of crucial importance to life on earth because they are the source of the rivers, which flow toward the sea, veining the land with essential lifeblood. Rivers have always been an important aspect of spiritual life. They were regarded by the sages as symbols of *samsara*, the endless cycle of birth and death. On the distant shore, liberation awaited those who were able to cross the river's turbulent waters with the ship of yoga. Rivers like the Ganges and Yamuna were looked upon as goddesses (*devis*) and graceful mothers (*mayis*), who embraced even their dirtiest children. Rivers have the power not only to carry the ashes of the deceased towards the heavens, but also to wash away the bad impressions left by a person's wrongdoings of the past.

Mountains are inseparable from rivers, which is why Himavat is also considered the father of Ganga Devi, the goddess of the Ganges, which is India's most sacred river.

## ꩜ The River of Life

Once King Bhagiratha prayed for Ganga to appear on earth and purify it. Ganga would only agree to descend from the heavenly

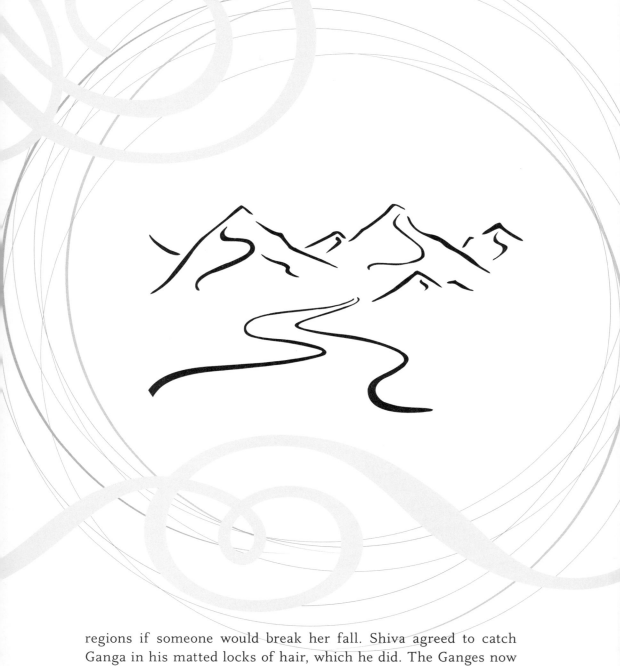

regions if someone would break her fall. Shiva agreed to catch Ganga in his matted locks of hair, which he did. The Ganges now rises from its source in the mountains where Shiva stood. When we stand in tadasana, the head, being nearest to heaven, is where we receive the blessings that flow through the rest of our body like a river.

# vrikshasana

## TREE POSE

*Vriksha* means "tree" in Sanskrit. The tree pose
is a standing balance on one leg. The foot of
the lifted leg is placed on the inner thigh of the
standing leg, and both hands are held above the
head, palms joined together. The legs represent
the roots of the tree, buried underground, and
the trunk of the tree begins at the trunk of the
body, growing all the way up through the spine
and the arms, which are the branches. This pose
enhances stability and strengthens the ankles,
calves, and thighs. It also stretches the muscles
of the legs, groin, and chest.

## ∽ The Yogi Tree

Since ancient times, yogis have made the forest their favorite place for yoga practice. The trees were their home, providing them with shelter and an abundance of food in the form of fruits and nuts. The forest also symbolized a pristine world that was conducive to a life of contemplation without material possessions. The shade beneath a tree was thought to be the best place for a student to receive spiritual knowledge from a teacher. In fact, among many spiritual traditions, we see examples of self-realization taking place under a tree.

In ancient times, there was a prayer that people recited when they took up residence on a patch of the forest. Freely translated, the prayer reads, "My dear trees, creepers, insects, and animals, please excuse me for taking a little piece of land to build my hut on. May we live together in harmony and peace." Many yogis and sages lived in the forest, where they built ashrams, or hermitages, usually consisting of some simple huts. The inhabited forest was known in Sanskrit as *tapovan*, or "forest of austerity," a reference to the life of simplicity lived there, free of worry about material belongings.

In a broader sense, the forest refers to the world, the whole of creation, and we are part of it. In the Bhagavad Gita, Krishna compares the world to a banyan tree with its many branches, where all species of life wander. A forest is vital for the planet's health. The leaves of the trees are the lungs of the world, producing oxygen for us to breathe, while the roots retain rainwater and prevent the soil from eroding.

## ～つ Forest of Grace

The tree pose offers a beautiful opportunity to meditate on a tree's inherent qualities. Sri Chaitanya, the dancing saint from Bengal, viewed tolerance, like that of a tree, as a prerequisite for attaining yoga. In one of his famous verses, Chaitanya sings, "Being more humble than a blade of grass, more tolerant than a tree, giving all honor to others, and not to want any honor for oneself—these are the qualities that are necessary for success in yoga." The tree is so tolerant that it even gives shade to the woodcutter who comes to cut it down with an axe. The true yogi freely gives the fruits of spiritual wisdom and love as generously as trees offer us shade, flowers, fruits, and wood.

Krishna has a special connection with the forest. He was born and raised in Vrindavan, which means "the forest of *vrinda* trees." In the Bhagavata Purana, Krishna praises the trees, exclaiming, "Just look at these most fortunate trees of Vrindavan. They have dedicated their lives to the welfare of others. Individually they tolerate all kinds of natural disturbances, torrents of rain, scorching heat, and piercing cold, but they are very careful to relieve our fatigue and give us shelter. My dear friends, no one is denied shelter by these trees. They supply various kinds of provisions for human society, such as leaves, flowers, fruit, shade, roots, bark, and fuel."

The tree pose is a posture in which we imbue body, mind, and breath with the qualities of generosity, forbearance, strength, and balance.

# gomukhasana

## COW FACE POSE

This posture is said to resemble the face (*mukh*) of a cow (*go*). From a seated position, the practitioner places one bent knee over the other, forming the cow's lips. One arm goes laterally behind the back, and the fingers grasp the fingers of the other arm, which is bent over the corresponding shoulder (forming the cow's ears). This asana tones and strengthens the ankles, hips, thighs, and shoulders.

## The Holy Cow

The cow is one of India's holiest animals. Cows are the kings of cool, roaming placidly in public places or standing in the middle of some highway, where cars, the holy cow of modern times, try to avoid hitting them at any cost. The cow is considered to be the giver of plenty. In India all of the cow's products are used: Its strength helps farmers plow the field; its urine is a strong antiseptic; its dung makes excellent fuel for stoves; and its milk yields butter and ghee. (Indians use the latter for both cooking and a variety of religious rituals.)

The cow is also the embodiment of different yogic qualities. Cows are very peaceful and down-to-earth. They are also generous and motherly and are in fact considered to be one of the universal mothers. When the mother cow sees her calf, her milk flows freely and abundantly. The relationship between the cow and her calf is therefore the perfect symbol for the relationship between the earth and its inhabitants. Like a calf, we can give the earth our love while using her gifts in a sustainable and wholesome way.

## Krishna, the Divine Cow Herder

Among Krishna's many names is Gopala, "the protector of the cows," and Govinda, "one who takes care of the cows." At one time, Brahma, the creator of the universe, sincerely doubted Krishna's divinity. He thought to himself, "How can this simple cow herder be an avatar of Vishnu? He is just a simple peasant boy. He has a flute tucked into his belt, and a peacock feather in his hair. And he walks barefoot in the forest!" Brahma decided to put Krishna to the test.

One fine day while Krishna was resting with his cowherd friends in the forest, Brahma kidnapped the cowherd boys and the calves and hid them in a cave. When Brahma returned to see how Krishna was reacting upon discovering his loss, he found, to his amazement, that Krishna was playing with all the cowherd boys and the calves he had just stolen. So Brahma went back to the cave, where he saw all the calves and boys he had originally hidden. Brahma looked with all four of his heads at the same time—at the cave and at Krishna—and saw that somehow all the calves and boys had doubles. Krishna had actually multiplied his very self into calves and cowherd boys to thwart Brahma.

Brahma had not understood this simple cow herder's divinity or his ability to be all things for all people. Krishna was able to be the cows for the cow herders, and the hidden cows and cow-herding boys for Brahma. And for us, the spirit of Krishna can be found in the form of anyone whose company we adore. The name Krishna literally means "all attractive." We can be attractive to another person by being what he or she needs—a son, daughter, coworker, or shoulder to cry on. While we are sitting in the cow-face pose, we are putting on another face, just as we might when we put our "all attractive" nature for the benefit of the people in our lives whom we adore.

# bakasana

## CRANE POSE

*Bakasana*, or crane pose, is an arm balance that looks like a crane standing in the water. It is performed by placing the hands on the ground, bending the elbows, and placing the knees on the backs of the arms. In this pose we need to fix our gaze on one spot (known as *dristhi*) to find the proper balance, like a crane that is completely focused on the water while fishing for its food.

## ~⌒ The God of Death Disguised as a Crane

The Mahabharata is an Indian epic that tells the tale of two families who were fighting for the right to rule the land: the righteous Pandava family, who were the underdogs, and their formidable foes, the wicked Kaurava family. The five Pandava brothers were defeated in a gambling game of dice by the Kauravas and were banished from their kingdom and exiled to the forest for twelve years. One day they were all thirsty and went to search for water. After climbing a tree, they spotted a lake, and one after another, the brothers went to fetch water. But each time a brother arrived at the lake, a loud voice warned that if he drank from it, he would die. The brothers were so thirsty, however, that they couldn't resist the refreshing drink. And so one after another, they died.

The last one to arrive at the lake was the eldest brother, King Yudhisthira. When the king saw that his four brothers were dead, he was grief stricken. Suddenly the voice spoke again, but this time Yudhisthira saw the speaker—a giant crane, which appeared in front of him. The crane said, "I am the one who killed your brothers. If you touch the water, you shall also die. But if you can answer all my questions correctly, I shall bring all your brothers back to life." And then the crane asked Yudhisthira the following questions:

"What is the news of the world?" To this question Yudhisthira did not reply with news about the economic situation or the latest natural disaster, which is what most news broadcasts today are filled with. Instead, Yudhisthira replied, "All living beings have forgotten their inner divine nature and find themselves in a state of ignorance, or *avidya*, which causes them to suffer."

The next question was, "What is the greatest wonder?" Again Yudhisthira didn't answer the obvious, like the pyramids of Egypt or the Taj Mahal. Instead he replied, "Although we see around us

that all people and other living creatures are constantly dying, we believe this will not happen to us. We think that somehow we will escape death."

The third question was, "What is the true path?" Yudhisthira answered, "The true path lies in following the saints and yogis who have achieved self-realization. The truth lies hidden in the caves of their hearts, and they will share their knowledge and grace with anyone who cares to receive it. By associating with those great teachers who have no egocentric attachments and live only to give, we will emulate those qualities."

And for his last question the crane asked, "Who is happy in this world?" To this Yudhisthira answered, "The self-realized person, who has cleared all his debts by resolving all of his or her *karma*, is truly happy." Finally the crane revealed himself as Yama, the god of death. He was very pleased by King Yudhisthira's answers and revived all his brothers.

These questions and their answers are a summary of the yogic path. It all begins with the realization that we often forget about our divine nature, which causes us to suffer. This ignorance is very strong and persistent, and we wrongly believe that death only happens to others. It causes us to mistakenly identify with our ever-changing body and mind. But after realizing our misunderstanding, we can take appropriate measures to alleviate it. We can start living a life based on the principles of yoga by reconnecting with our true self. The more we connect with our divine nature, the more we experience lasting peace and fulfillment. This is the promise of yoga, open for all of us to experience right here and now.

King Yudhisthira did not lose his balance when confronted with the demise of his brothers and the challenging task of answering the crane's probing questions. We, too, are invited to keep our balance while focusing in bakasana.

# shavasana

## CORPSE POSE

Shavasana is the final resting pose, in which we lie down on our back and relax the whole body in order to absorb the effects of the practice we just engaged in. *Shavasana* literally means "corpse pose." It symbolizes the death of the ego and the promise of awakening to an enlightened state of consciousness.

In Western cultures most people consider death the ultimate downer and tend to avoid the subject as much as possible. In the yoga tradition however, death is not viewed with such displeasure. It is the final rite of passage that prepares us for the promise of a new tomorrow. As Krishna explains to Arjuna in the Bhagavad Gita, the physical body is the clothing of our soul, which needs to be changed when it has worn out. In the story of *bakasana*, we saw that we often do not think about our own impending death. The yoga tradition suggests that it would be wise to consider it, because it gives us a sense of purpose that can inspire us to make good use of the time we have on earth.

## An Elegant End

There once lived a king named Parikshit Maharaj. He was a wise and just ruler and always took good care of his subjects. It so happened that one day the king was riding through the woods when he became thirsty. So he stopped at the hermitage of the sage Shamika Rishi and asked the yogi for some water. But Shamika Rishi was in a state of deep mediation, and he did not hear the king's request. Parikshit Maharaj became annoyed and threw a dead snake that was lying on the ground around the neck of the meditating sage. Just then the sage's son appeared. Seeing how the king had insulted his father, he cursed Parikshit, announcing that he would die from a snake bite in seven days.

When Shamika Rishi came out of his meditation and found out what happened, he rebuked his son for having cursed an honorable king for such a minor offense. However, once spoken, the curse could not be undone. Accepting his fate, King Parikshit went home and gave up his throne. Then he went to the bank of the Ganges, where an assembly of sages had gathered to meditate and discuss

spiritual topics. King Parikshit arrived and asked the sages to teach him about the science of yoga.

Just then, a sixteen-year-old naked sage named Sukadeva arrived. As the son of Vyasa, the compiler of the entire Vedic literature, Sukadeva was completely self-realized. All the sages stood up and paid respect to him. Then King Parikshit requested that Sukadeva instruct him on the science of the soul. For the next seven days, Sukadeva taught the king about yoga. During these teachings, it was so silent you could hear a pin drop. When Sukadeva asked the king if he would like to pause for some food and drink, the king replied that the divine knowledge was fully satisfying his hunger and thirst. After seven days, the king achieved self-realization and welcomed his physical death with an open heart and mind.

## Transcending Death

King Parikshit made a remarkable choice when he knew his death was near and unavoidable. Instead of spending his last days with his family or enjoying his riches, he chose to retire to the forest and meditate on yoga amid an assembly of sages. What would we do if we knew we only had seven days left to live?

Parakshit Maharaj was actually very fortunate, because he knew exactly when he was going to die. He had a guaranteed seven days to live and made good use of them. We, on the other hand, have no idea when our time will come. As King Yudhisthira explained in the story of bakasana, it is illusion (*maya*) that causes us to deny our own mortality. But is there any assurance that we will live long enough to see another sunrise? Death is the ultimate wake-up call. When it comes, we have to leave behind all we have accumulated. We come into this world with empty hands, and we must leave with empty hands. Being conscious of death in a yogic way does not turn us into curmudgeons, but instead allows us to live every moment in freedom and joy.

Shavasana represents the surrender of all things that are foreign to our soul. When we have completed our yoga practice and given it our best, it is time to let go. The moment has come for yoga nidra, the yogic sleep. It is not born out of tiredness and is instead a completely open state of mind and heart that invites the grace of unconditional love into our life. Krishna, as the embodiment of that love, says to Arjuna in the Bhagavad Gita, "Please give up all your duties and surrender unto me as love personified. I promise that when you die, you will come to me, and will not be born again in the world of illusion. This knowledge is the supreme wisdom and the most secret of all secrets. It is the purest knowledge, it is imperishable, and its experience brings the greatest joy."

# afterword

WE ALL HAVE THE TOOLS to expand our yogic experience; we need only to properly access them and allow them to move through us. The myth behind each asana is the link that helps the practitioner properly understand a pose and increase the mental and spiritual benefits of yoga beyond the physical postures.

*Myths of the Asanas* offers the reader an opportunity to journey into this metaphoric link that exists between the yoga pose and its myths. When one engages an asana, one can explore not only the literal pose but also the depth contained in the pose's story. This fluid linking between the ancient and the modern gives the student of yoga both a window into the profound yogic path as well as a manageable lesson to practice with.

Through storytelling, we are enabled to enter the realm of the gods for a time and live amongst them. Once we feel deeply rooted and understand the meaning of a story, it becomes us. This book reminds us of the importance of properly understanding ourselves and the world around us, for when we feel that pure joy inside, we can share it with others. In effect, Alanna Kaivalya and Arjuna van der Kooji are saying, "Inspire others to find the source of joy by living that joy."

Engaging the asana enables the student to gain access to the principles contained in the teachings of yoga. When one enacts *anjali mudra*, for example, the actual feeling of reverence emerges within, and one is unknowingly linked with the respectful action that brought about the pose. Through *chakrasana* one discovers the energetic wheels that exist within the body. With this newfound awareness, the student has an opportunity to become familiar with the beauty of the *chakra* system overall and to align with the natural balance that exists at the center of our being.

Asanas themselves become animate in this book and act almost as gurus. Through the seemingly simple act of stepping into a pose, one is invited to access the profound myths and wisdom contained in them. When our practice of the pose matures and merges with our understanding of its myth, we experience the true meaning of our practice, which is peace and alignment in this very life.

MANORAMA
*January 2010*

# acknowledgements

### FROM ALANNA KAIVALYA, PH.D

First and foremost, dearest thanks go to my co-author and literary knight in shining armor, Arjuna Van der Kooij. His depth of knowledge and elevation of spirit were an inspiration as we worked together. Many humble thanks to my greatest teachers, Sharon Gannon, David Life, and Manorama. Without their guidance and teachings, as well as the insights of a great many others, my path would not be supported by both roots and wings. To my right hand men, Mark Meiners and Cory Bryant, who literally went to the ends of the earth for me in this process, I offer great love. Finally, to the greatest friend I could ever ask for, Chris Yeazel, without whom I wouldn't have had the courage to keep stepping into bigger shoes.

### FROM ARJUNA VAN DER KOOIJ

I wish to thank my teachers for passing on the priceless gift of yoga; Raoul Goff for his friendship, vision, and inspiration; Zach Kaufher for his critical eye and poetic contribution; Ineke Willeboordse and Stefan Bakker for their editorial feedback; and all the people at Mandala for publishing beautiful and meaningful books. Much gratitude and love to all my family and friends who are a source of continuous joy. And my deepest appreciation to co-author and buddy Alanna Kaivalya for making this project such an inspiring and joyful journey.

The authors would also like to thank the long line of teachers who have told and retold the stories in this book in ever-fresh ways; Raoul Goff for getting the ball rolling; Jake Gerli for laying the groundwork to bring this book to life; copyeditors Deborah Kops and Mikayla Butchart for helping to polish our words; designers Dagmar Trojanek and Barbara Genetin for creating the book's elegant look; production manager Anna Wan for making sure the finished product was first-class; thanks to Jan Brzezinski and Phillip Jones for their kind suggestions; Shiva Rea for her wonderful foreword; Manorama for her equally wonderful afterword; Rusty "Gopa" Wells, Ana Forrest and Rodney Yee for their kind endorsements; and finally, the lovely and amazing Kevin Toyama, our managing magician and editorial wrangler.